Courtroom Skills
for Social Workers

Courtroom Skills for Social Workers

CLARE AND RICHARD SEYMOUR

Series Editors:
Jonathan Parker and Greta Bradley

LearningMatters

First published in 2007 by Learning Matters Ltd
Reprinted in 2009

British Library Cataloguing in Publication Data
A CIP record for this book is available from the British Library.

ISBN 978 1 84445 123 4

Cover and text design by Code 5 Design Associates Ltd
Project Management by Deer Park Productions, Tavistock, Devon
Typeset by Pantek Arts Ltd, Maidstone, Kent
Printed and bound in Great Britain by Cromwell Press Group, Trowbridge, Wiltshire

Learning Matters Ltd
33 Southernhay East
Exeter EX1 1 NX
Tel: 01392 215560
info@learningmatters.co.uk
www.learningmatters.co.uk

Contents

Acknowledgements

We have received valuable assistance from people who undertake different roles in court settings, and we especially express our warmest thanks to the following:

Barbara Armitage, Dave Barron, Chris Beckett, Christopher Compston, Hazel Davies, Amy Gordon, Alison Lamont, Greg Mantle, Ann Milne, Dot Neville, John Noyce and Valerie Pearlman.

We are also very grateful to our partners-in-authorship, Ken Johnson and Isabel Williams, for their support and encouragement.

Introduction

This book is for any social worker or social work degree student who is interested in developing their courtroom skills. It will enable you to meet the QAA subject benchmarks for social work, and the national occupational standards for social work listed at the start of each chapter address the legislative framework requirements of the Department of Health and also meets GSCC specialist standards and requirements for post-qualifying social work education and training in relation to work with children, young people, their families and carers (GSCC, 2005).

Commentators have suggested that relationships between lawyers and social workers can be strained, characterised by mistrust or even antagonism (Preston-Shoot et al., 1998, cited in SCIE, 2005; Dickens, 2006), and that social workers often regard the law as intimidating, confrontational and more likely to be obstructive than empowering (Preston-Shoot, 2000). Despite the shared commitment to justice, fairness, honesty and transparency, many social workers feel uncomfortable about perceived differences in the professional value bases of law and social work, and indeed the need to invoke the law at all to resolve social issues. Recent studies (Dickens, 2006; Beckett et al., 2007) have also shown that social workers feel that court proceedings can seem like a game, in which the service user's needs become sidelined or obscured. Our aim is to demystify court processes and encourage you to see involvement with the courts as a positive element of your practice rather than something to be afraid of or defended against (SCIE, 2005). In helping you become more confident and, if necessary, critical, we hope that this will also result in you being better equipped to support service users who are faced with court involvement.

Chapter 1 explores the historical development of the law, and shows that the way in which the English legal system has developed historically can explain some of its more obscure or apparently illogical concepts.

Chapter 2 describes the English legal system in practice, offering an 'insider view' of the courts, law officers and the relationships between them, including legal training, statistics, how cases are presented in court, alternative dispute resolution and proposed future developments.

Chapter 3 focuses on comparing and contrasting the values and principles which underpin law and social work and encourages you to take advantage of the opportunities and challenges they present. We explore confidentiality, conflict of interest, fairness, anti-discriminatory practice and partnership and how lawyers approach problems. Differences in personal attributes and career motivation on the part of lawyers and social workers are also considered.

Chapter 4 explains legal language and concepts, including types and sources of law, the people you will find in court and types of hearing. It also includes definitions of the most common legal terms.

Chapter 5 outlines important court rules, including hearsay, disclosure and inspection of documents, public interest immunity, legal professional privilege, litigation privilege, without prejudice communications and the evidence of children and vulnerable witnesses.

Chapter 6 discusses how to prepare for court, including taking and using legal advice, communicating with lawyers and other professionals, confidentiality, reports and files, what to wear, support for the client and practical arrangements.

Chapter 7 addresses report writing and looks at case recordings, statements, duty to the court, what to include, supporting analysis and opinion with facts, achieving clarity of language, demonstrating respect and how to present your report.

Chapter 8 prepares you for what to expect at court, including pre-hearing consultations and negotiations, confidentiality, court layout, how to address judges and magistrates, the order in which things happen, the atmosphere in court and how proceedings are recorded and reported.

Chapter 9 explores giving evidence, including the social worker's status as witness, when and how to enter the witness box, the oath, whether to sit or stand, volume and speed, additions to your witness statement, body language, relevance, interruptions to the evidence, changes and additions and relations with other parties.

Chapter 10 considers cross-examination, including its purpose, what you are likely to be asked about, how advocates approach cross-examination and types of question, and offers a range of strategies for handling cross-examination.

Chapter 11 looks at legal decision-making and appeals, including what makes a good judge, deciding the facts and applying the law, assessing witnesses and the burden of proof.

Chapter 12 describes the system of tribunals, panels and inquiries which are due for significant reform in the future.

Chapter 13 is concerned with legal advice and representation. We explore public funding of legal costs and possible alternative way of obtaining legal advice and representation, including advocacy and McKenzie friends, in relation to both criminal and civil law proceedings.

Chapter 14 focuses on what happens after the court proceedings are over. We discuss first reactions, encourage reflection, and consider ways in which you can develop assertiveness. Finally, and most importantly, the needs of service users are considered against a framework of the potential losses they may face as a consequence of court decisions.

Throughout the book, there are activities, diagrams, case studies, vignettes and comments from people who have court work experience in a variety of roles. All are intended to offer practical information and advice, and to encourage your continuing professional development through reflection and critical analysis of court processes and your own experience.

Chapter 1
The English legal system in context

ACHIEVING A SOCIAL WORK DEGREE

This chapter addresses the subject knowledge and understanding of the service delivery context defined within QAA subject benchmarks for social work, and will help you meet the following national occupational standard for social work:

Key role 6: Demonstrate professional competence in social work practice.
- Review and update your own knowledge of legal, policy and procedural frameworks.

Introduction

> *As English law embarks on a period of radical reform and challenge, its longer-term history is becoming an increasingly important topic.*
>
> (Baker, 2002, p1)

Part of the apprehension which non-lawyers feel when involved with legal processes stems from lack of familiarity with, and understanding of, the English legal system. Not only is its terminology obscure, but the way in which it has developed has produced a system which can seem alien and illogical. In explaining the present organisation of our courts and legal profession, we are reminded of the proverbial advice to the lost motorist: *If I were you, I wouldn't start from here*. The United Kingdom of Great Britain and Northern Ireland comprises the four countries, England, Wales, Scotland and Northern Ireland. So why is there not a United Kingdom legal system? Or a British legal system? As so often in puzzling aspects of national life, the answers lie in history.

ACTIVITY 1.1

Review your current knowledge, skills and learning needs.

- *Where has your present knowledge of the English legal system come from?*

- *What experiences have you had of English law generally?*

- *What experiences have you had of the legal framework of social work?*

- *What do you think will help you develop confidence in working within a legal framework?*

English common law

You probably think of law as something which results from Parliament having debated an issue and then passed an Act. However, before the Norman invasion of England in 1066, law did not exist in the form in which it does now. England, Wales, Scotland and Ireland were then separate countries, and laws in England, such as they were, were more like customs, developed to regulate society. Different parts of the country produced different laws and customs, partly because during the previous Anglo-Saxon period England was divided into several kingdoms. In 1066, what we think of as the law was not regarded as distinct from other aspects of society. Local courts, which had existed since Anglo-Saxon times, dealt with all forms of public business, including settling disputes and punishing offenders. However, successive Norman kings, starting with Henry II, decided to set up central, royal courts, concerned only with the administration of justice. The courts which developed as a result were the predecessors of the courts we have today, which explains both why the legal system is as it is and some of the unusual names still in use.

The decision to have central courts also explains how English law has developed. In order to operate effectively, the royal courts needed to have one legal system in place of the variety of local laws and customs. It was necessary, therefore, to have a *common law* which applied to everyone, which is how English common law came about. For lawyers, *common law* has a number of meanings. As we have seen, historically it is the law applicable to the whole of England. In another sense, however, it is law which is not written down in Acts of Parliament, but which is found in the decisions of judges over the last thousand years. Not surprisingly, records for the earlier part of that period are sketchy, but since the sixteenth century judges' decisions have been recorded in books called law reports. A decision made five hundred years ago is not often referred to today, but it does sometimes happen. Because this part of our law is based on custom, in theory it has always been the same, which means that when judges decide a case on the principles of the English common law, they are not making new law, but are revealing what the law has always been.

ACTIVITY *1.2*

Donoghue *v.* Stevenson *[1932] AC 562*

Look up the details of this case (which involves a snail and a bottle of lemonade) in a law library or on the internet. Although it dates back more than seventy years, the Appeal Court's decision established a legal principle which still stands today.

The existence of English common law, in the sense of law which is not contained in Acts of Parliament, has had two effects which are important to the development of the English legal system:

- unlike almost every other country, the United Kingdom has no written constitution; and

- the most fundamental principles of English law are not found in Acts of Parliament, but in decisions of judges.

A written constitution usually includes the creation of a court system, provision for the appointment of judges and a definition of their powers. The Acts of Parliament which deal with various courts and tribunals in England are all fairly recent in the context of their history; the first to deal with the higher courts was passed in 1873, 700 years after the first attempts to establish a central court system. All of the Acts of Parliament which affect what is now the High Court have been passed on the assumption that that court has what is called *inherent jurisdiction*. This means no more than the jurisdiction which the predecessors of the High Court had always had. But to discover what this is, again we need to look at their history.

In countries like France or Germany, where all laws are written down or *codified*, the function of judges is limited to interpreting the law and applying it to the facts of a particular case. However, in England, because so much important law is not found in Acts of Parliament, and because the powers of the High Court are not precisely defined, the role of judges in the High Court is possibly more important than that of judges in countries with codified laws. There is one important exception, however; in countries with a written constitution, there is sometimes a court, like the Supreme Court of the United States of America, which has the power to overrule, as being unconstitutional, laws passed by the equivalent of Parliament. No court in England has that power.

The third sense in which lawyers use the expression common law is to distinguish between the type of law called equity and law which is not equity, but in this context common law can, confusingly, include statute. We shall look at equity later in this chapter.

The development of central courts – the initial stages

In the early Middle Ages, the principle became established that the source of justice was the king, who consequently had to ensure that justice was delivered to his citizens. This was partly achieved by the king taking control of local courts, but a system also developed of officials being sent around the country to supervise royal officials, collect taxes and settle grievances. In 1178 Henry II, deciding that he needed to have permanent officials to decide disputes, set up a group of five members of his household, two of whom were clergymen, whom he instructed to *hear all the complaints of the realm and to do right*. This body then evolved into a permanent court, the Court of Common Pleas. The name *court* came from those assembled round the king, his court, and *pleas* simply meant claims. Although no longer used in this sense, the word *plea* is still used in criminal courts to indicate whether defendants admit their guilt or not. *Common* meant between subjects of the king, rather than cases in which the king had an interest. Initially, the Court of Common Pleas had to refer difficult cases to the king for him to decide, in consultation with what were called the wiser men of the realm, and so in effect it was possible to appeal to the king against a decision of the Court of Common Pleas.

In addition to the cases referred to the king and the wiser men of the realm, there were also referrals of disputes which involved the king. It was inconvenient for the king personally to be involved in all these decisions, and so, by the beginning of Edward I's reign, these types of case were dealt with by a group of professional judges, called the Court of King's Bench. The name came from the fact that the judges were exercising the king's functions as the ultimate judge of the country. The court had close relations with the king's council, and the king himself continued to be involved with its decisions until the reign of Edward III. The role of the king as the ultimate judge explains, as we shall see, why the final court of appeal at the time of writing is the House of Lords, which has taken over the king's judicial functions in hearing appeals.

The Court of Common Pleas and the Court of King's Bench no longer exist. They and the third common law court, the Court of Exchequer, which was concerned originally with financial matters, were amalgamated in 1873 into what is now the High Court. At first, each of these former courts survived as a Division of the High Court, and as Queen Victoria was on the throne, the Court of King's Bench became the Court of Queen's Bench. In 1881 the three divisions were amalgamated into the Queen's Bench Division, which remains one of the Divisions of the High Court. Although originally the Courts of Common Pleas and King's Bench travelled around the country as the king progressed from place to place, they soon became based permanently in Westminster, and the higher courts remained in Westminster Hall until the Royal Courts of Justice opened in the Strand, London in 1882.

Deciding the facts in the Court of Common Pleas was entrusted to juries, and it was considered necessary for the members of the jury to come from the county where the particular dispute arose. Initially, once the Court of Common Pleas became established in Westminster, each jury had to go there. However, it soon became clear that it was easier to send the judges to the jury. Other types of judicial business, in particular serious criminal trials, also involved judges travelling around the country, and so the judges sent out from the Court of Common Pleas began to undertake all the necessary business in the county to which they were despatched, which was the origin of the *assize system*. The judges conducted hearings outside London in assize towns, which were, at the time, the principal towns of the country. Today High Court judges still sit in Crown Courts in some of the old assize towns, such as Lewes in Sussex, which are now less important places than cities quite close to them. During the Middle Ages, travel was not especially easy, and it made sense for judges to visit other places in the area before returning to London. In most parts of the country there was a logical progression from London to the various assize towns and then back to London, which is how assize circuits developed. The country is still divided for legal purposes into circuits, of which there are now six. Most barristers are members of a circuit, which still have some significance for the administration of the courts and the assignment of judges to particular areas.

It is unlikely that Henry II was motivated to offer the first national judicial service by purely philanthropic sentiments; it also gave him the opportunity to charge fees, and was a way of showing and exercising his power throughout the country at a time when there were plenty of powerful barons about.

Judges appointed in the reign of Henry II were referred to as *justices* and High Court judges are still called *Mr Justice* or *Mrs Justice*. For some reason the title *Miss Justice* for unmarried female judges has never been used.

Juries

The jury as we know it today is quite different from the origins of the jury. The jury's current role is to hear the evidence and decide the facts in a criminal trial in the Crown Court or, sometimes, at an inquest or, more rarely, in a civil trial of a libel, slander or false arrest or false imprisonment action. Originally juries were not meant to be independent assessors of evidence; they were summoned because they were supposed to have prior knowledge of the facts.

The jury replaced previous methods of deciding whether a person charged with a serious offence was guilty, which was to subject them to an ordeal, a wager of law or trial by battle. None of the ordeals involved making a rational assessment of guilt, and all involved subjecting accused people to disagreeable tasks and seeing whether they survived without lasting damage. Wager of law was in effect a local popularity contest, while trial by battle speaks for itself.

Until the end of the nineteenth century, juries decided the facts in both civil and criminal cases. They have lost this role in respect of most civil cases, and the function which they still have in libel cases and other limited categories is all that is left of a much more influential role in the justice system.

Coroners

If you have ever wondered why there has to be a coroner's inquest into sudden or suspicious deaths, or how coroners came to be involved with questions of treasure trove, the answer is money. Citizens were potentially liable to a fine if a Norman died in unexplained circumstances, and the coroner's original function was to ensure that the king received any fines due to him as a result of such deaths, and any abandoned treasure to which he was also entitled.

Local criminal courts and the origin of magistrates

Most people are familiar with magistrates' courts as the lowest level of court, and know that those who preside over them are often referred to as justices of the peace, a title dating back to the Justices of the Peace Act 1361, passed during the Hundred Years War with France. During a break in the fighting, English soldiers were demobilised and started roaming the country causing trouble, and the original justices of the peace were worthy local citizens appointed in each district to restore and maintain order. Originally they received salaries payable from the fines they imposed, but as their value declined, the salaries were not worth collecting and so they have long been obsolete. Whether that fact is relevant or not, justices of the peace were considered to do such a good job in dealing with crime at a local level that they have continued to carry out the same functions for nearly 650 years.

Because justices of the peace had no legal qualifications, their jurisdiction and powers were limited. However, they were not only a court. Before elected county and district councils were established at the end of the nineteenth century, local government was managed by justices of the peace, who met four times a year to decide important matters at *quarter sessions*, which came also to include legal business. They sat with a legally qualified chairman and had more powers than when they were sitting alone, in what were called *petty sessions*.

Chancery

One of the present Divisions of the High Court is the Chancery Division, the origin of which was the Court of Chancery, incorporated into the High Court in 1873. The word *Chancery* is a contraction of *Chancellery*, the department of the Chancellor, or, in England, the Lord Chancellor. Under the Constitutional Reform Act 2005, the Lord Chancellor has ceased to be head of the judiciary, a function which he had had for some 900 years. How did he come to have that role in the first place?

The Lord Chancellor was always an important royal official as Keeper of the King's Conscience. At that time, it was really only clergymen who were literate, so most civil servants were clergymen. The Courts of Common Pleas and King's Bench were both what is called *common law courts*, in that the law applied in them was the English common law. In time, the way in which cases were dealt with came to depend on compliance with strict rules and you could lose a case because you had not followed the rules correctly, even if your case was otherwise a good one. People thought this was unfair, and some complained to the king. The Lord Chancellor, in his role as Keeper of the King's Conscience, developed an approach to disputes which ignored the strict rules and concentrated on what was thought to be fair or *equitable*. Initially it was said that what the Lord Chancellor decided was equitable varied with the length of his foot; in other words, there were no set principles or consistency. However, gradually the rules became more standardised and known as *equity*. Like English common law rules, they are not written down, but are found in cases reported in law reports. The court in which a person could seek equity was the Lord Chancellor's Court, the Court of Chancery. In effect, equity trumped common law rights, and you could go to the Court of Chancery to obtain an order preventing someone from taking advantage of a common law right in a common law court, which was useful in some cases.

The ecclesiastical courts and the origins of the Family Division

In the Middle Ages, the state did not concern itself with family matters. Marriage, the ending of marriage and the consequences of death were of no interest to the king, except in relation to the passing of property rights, which affected the operation of the feudal system. At first, grants of land by the king to lords were for life only and the land reverted to the king on the lord's death. However, later, landowners could leave their property to whomever they liked. The state had no continuing interest in this, and so marriage, the ending of marriage and wills were all dealt with by the church. At that time marriage was for life and there was no possibility of divorce. A marriage could be annulled, but the process was complicated and expensive. Disputes about these matters were determined in church courts, which still exist within the Church of England, although they now have limited jurisdiction in relation to clergymen and church buildings. The church courts did not apply the English common law or the principles of equity to resolving disputes, but principles derived from the law of the church. This meant the law of the Roman Catholic Church, which applied throughout Western Europe, and was heavily influenced by the law of the Romans.

Starting from the Reformation in the reign of Henry VIII, the state became more interested in matters which had been left to the church courts. First, wills came into the sphere of the Court of Chancery. In the eighteenth century Parliament started to intervene in regulating marriage, which was followed by legislation governing how wills should be made. An Act of Parliament permitting divorce in very limited circumstances was passed in 1857, and a divorce court was established, which was amalgamated into the High Court in 1873 as part of what was then known as the Probate, Divorce and Admiralty Division, but which is now the Family Division. From 1857 onwards family matters came increasingly within the jurisdiction of the ordinary courts.

County Courts

County courts existed in Anglo-Saxon times, but the modern county courts were established by the County Courts Act 1846. At first, anyone wanting to pursue a civil claim, no matter how modest the amount involved, had to start the action in London, which was very inconvenient. Local county courts, with limited jurisdiction, were therefore introduced to deal with the recovery of small debts and demands. Over time, the jurisdiction of county courts has been increased and they now deal with a wide range of civil matters.

The Crown Court

After the creation of the High Court, judges of the Queen's Bench Division and the Probate, Divorce and Admiralty Division, but not the Chancery Division, continued to try serious criminal cases at assizes. Cases which were less serious, but still too serious to be tried in the magistrates' court, were tried by quarter sessions. These two systems were combined by the Courts Act 1971, which established Crown Courts, where all serious criminal cases are now tried. High Court judges of the Queen's Bench and Family Divisions preside over the most serious cases.

The Court of Appeal

The Civil Division of the Court of Appeal was established by the Judicature Act 1873. Before this, a number of courts had heard appeals from other courts, but from then all appeals from the county and High Courts were heard by one court. This situation has been altered recently, and most appeals from county courts are now heard by a High Court judge. When it was created, the Court of Appeal did not hear appeals in criminal cases and the Court of Criminal Appeal was established in 1907. In 1968, the Court of Criminal Appeal merged with the Court of Appeal, which now has Civil and Criminal Divisions, with the same judges sitting in either division as required.

The House of Lords

The role of the House of Lords as a court, as well as part of Parliament, dates back to when the king was the fount of all justice, and if you thought someone had done you a wrong, the person who could put it right for you was the king. Now, however, supreme power is vested in Parliament, which has taken over the role of the monarch, not only in relation to making new laws, but also as the source of redress for anyone who feels that they have not achieved justice through other courts. The ultimate court of appeal is therefore Parliament, specifically the House of Lords. In time, the non-legally qualified members of the House of Lords came to appreciate that they should defer to those with appropriate legal knowledge and experience. Initially, they consulted the judges before making decisions, but later judges were made Law Lords in order to deal with the legal business which came to the House. At first, non-legal members could also take part, but from 1881 only judges appointed to the House of Lords could decide cases, which is the position as this book is being written. However, the Constitutional Reform Act 2005 provides for the creation of a Supreme Court to replace the House of Lords, which will then be the ultimate court of appeal, with no direct connection with the House of Lords. The Supreme Court is due to open for business in 2009.

ACTIVITY 1.3

What does a comparison of the historical development of our legal and social welfare systems (see Figure 1.1) tell you about the differences and similarities between them?

What effects, if any, do you think these historical influences are likely to have on the way the legal and social work professions operate today?

Advocates

The combination of the complexity of the rules to be followed to obtain a remedy in the common law courts, the particular rules of the Court of Chancery and the limited literacy of most citizens meant that people came forward to help litigants to present their cases. Initially they offered their services free, but it soon became expected that helpers should receive a reward from grateful litigants, although in theory this was not a fee but an *honorarium*, or gift. These litigants' helpers were the forerunners of the modern barristers, and barristers' gowns still have a small flap on the back from which a tape runs across the shoulder to hang down the front. This flap was originally a bag on a tape which barristers held out behind them in court in order to receive the present from the grateful client. The principle that barristers acted for free and only received a gift from their client prevailed until recently, and barristers could not sue for unpaid fees. However, the principle was moderated by the fact that it was professional misconduct for solicitors who instructed barristers not to pay them the agreed fee.

Local customs and laws	before	1000	
		1100	
Court of Common Pleas		1200	
Juries			
Court of King's Bench		1300	
Court of Exchequer			
Assize System established			
Litigants' helpers appeared			
1361 Justices of the Peace Act		1400	
		1500	
Law Reports record judges' decisions			
		1600	1601 Poor Law – parishes responsible for own poor; 'deserving' v. 'undeserving'
		1700	
		1800	1795 Berkshire magistrates devised Speenhamland system of poor relief based on wage level, marital status, number of children and price of bread
1845 Law Society founded			1834 Poor Law Amendment Act
1846 County Courts established			required parishes to build workhouses
1857 First Divorce Court			with strict regimes
1873 High Court and Court of Appeal established			1869 Charity Organisation Society
1876 First Law Lords appointed			1871 Poor Law Board became part of local government
1882 Royal Courts of Justice opened			
1894 General Council of the Bar founded			1889 Prevention of Cruelty to Children Act
1907 Court of Criminal Appeal established		1900	1907 Probation of Offenders Act
			1933 Children and Young Persons Act
			1948 Children Act, National Assistance Act and Welfare State
1968 Court of Criminal Appeal merged into Court of Appeal			1954 First generic social work course
			1970 Local Authority Social Services Act
1971 Crown Courts established			1971 CCETSW set up to regulate social work training
		2000	2000 Care Standards Act, GSCC set up
Supreme Court to be established			to regulate social work profession

Figure 1.1 Development of legal and social welfare systems

Once a profession of litigants' helpers – barristers – became established, they had to be trained and regulated, which led to the establishment of the Inns of Court. Aspiring barristers had to show that they were suitable for acceptance by the Inn and discipline was exercised by senior members, who were usually judges, known as Masters of the Bench or Benchers. From the seventeenth century, the right to appear as an advocate in the Royal Courts was restricted to members of an Inn. The surviving Inns of Court are the Inner Temple, the Middle Temple, Lincoln's Inn and Gray's Inn, which have been in their present locations in London since the sixteenth century. The Inns also provided, and still do to an extent, residential and professional accommodation for their members. The Inner Temple and the Middle Temple are on the site of the Priory of the Knights Templar, known as the Temple, between Fleet Street and the Thames.

As compared with barristers, solicitors are newcomers on the legal scene, although they had respectable predecessors, scriveners and attorneys. In the United States of America, the term attorney is still used for any type of practising lawyer, but it is no longer used in that sense in England. Towards the end of the eighteenth century solicitors emerged as the dominant branch of the non-advocacy part of the legal profession. Their function was to prepare formal legal documents, give legal advice and instruct barristers to appear as advocates in court, or to give specialist advice. They were, and still are, the first port of call for people seeking legal advice in most circumstances. Originally, anyone who wanted to be represented or advised by a barrister first had to consult a solicitor. There are now various exceptions to that rule, but most people who are represented in court by a barrister will first have consulted a solicitor. Formerly it was unusual for solicitors to appear as advocates in court and they had no right to appear, or *right of audience*, in the higher courts. Now solicitors can qualify as advocates and present cases in the higher courts.

Why is the legal system, and the law, English?

Wales was not part of the territories governed by the king of England until the end of the thirteenth century and was not therefore involved in the earlier development of the English common law or in the initial establishment of courts in England. After the Battle of Bosworth Field in 1485, the Tudor dynasty, which had origins in Wales, came to the English throne. It was felt in Wales that, in respect of legal processes, the Welsh were disadvantaged as compared with the English and so, in a notable act of positive discrimination, Henry VIII, the second Tudor king, persuaded Parliament to make Wales part of England by law. From the end of the thirteenth century, therefore, English law was applied in Wales in place of the preceding customary law, and for legal purposes Wales has been part of England since 1536.

From 1603 the king, or queen, of Scotland was also king, or queen, of England, but the monarchies were not united, and the kingdoms were separate until 1707. Scotland had therefore developed its own legal system, based on Roman law and its own court structure. Neither of these was altered when the kingdoms became united, which has remained the position ever since, except that the House of Lords is the final court of appeal in Scotland as it is in England. This is why English law is the law of England and Wales, but not the law of Scotland, and the court structure in England and Wales is different from that in Scotland.

Ireland was first invaded from England, or, more accurately, from Wales, in 1169. From then on a presence of Normans, English and Welsh eventually spread over the whole country, and English law was applied to the parts of Ireland controlled by the English king. The law which applied in Ireland was modified by laws passed when there was a Parliament in Dublin, but in 1801 Ireland joined the United Kingdom. For the next 120 years, Parliament in London passed laws applicable only to Ireland as well as laws which applied throughout the United Kingdom. In 1922, the Republic of Ireland became independent and Northern Ireland is the only part remaining in the United Kingdom. At times it has had its own Parliament and passed its own laws, but, as in the case of the Republic of Ireland, the laws and the structure of its courts remain similar to those of England. These laws are not English law, however, and therefore the next chapter is about the legal system of England and Wales.

CHAPTER SUMMARY

This chapter has described the historical development of the courts and legal system in England and Wales and explained why we do not have a United Kingdom legal system. In comparing the development of the legal system with that of our social welfare system, it is possible to see why the law is still fairly strongly rooted in tradition. Significant development took place in both areas during Victorian times, which for social welfare continued throughout the twentieth century. Courts and the legal profession, having had a fairly stable period over the past thirty years, are now facing significant change, against a background of concerns about rising costs and demands for more transparent accountability.

FURTHER READING

Baker, J. H. (2002) *An Introduction to English Legal History*, 4th edn. London: Butterworths.
This text traces the development of the principal features of the English legal system.

Chapter 2

The English legal system in practice

A C H I E V I N G   A   S O C I A L   W O R K   D E G R E E

This chapter addresses the service delivery context defined within QAA subject benchmarks for social work, and will help you meet the following national occupational standards for social work:

Key role 1: Prepare for, and work with, individuals, families, carers, groups and communities to assess their needs and circumstances.

- Assess needs, risks and options taking into account legal and other requirements.

Key role 6: Demonstrate professional competence in social work practice.

- Review and update your own knowledge of legal, policy and procedural frameworks.

Introduction

Here we explore the nature of courts, lawyers and the relationships between them, encouraging you to develop an ability to undertake an informed and critical assessment of the English legal system. We also briefly consider future developments.

Organisation of the courts

ACTIVITY **2.1**

Review your current knowledge and learning needs.

- *What experience have you had of courts?*

- *In which area of court work do you feel most confident?*

- *In which area do you feel least confident?*

- *In what circumstances have you wished you knew more about courts?*

- *What do you think will help you develop confidence in working in a court environment?*

- *What barriers do you think you may face in developing courtroom skills?*

The English legal system is big business. Her Majesty's Courts Service (HMCS), an executive agency of the Department for Constitutional Affairs, took over management of the court system in England and Wales in 2005, has over 20,000 staff and is responsible for the work of more than 30,000 magistrates and judges, plus supporting staff. There are 116,000 solicitors, nearly half of them female, and more than 14,000 practising barristers, of whom around one third are female. Currently around 10 per cent of each profession is from minority ethnic groups.

HMCS operates through seven regions and 42 areas and its stated aims are:

> *All citizens according to their differing needs are entitled to access to justice, whether as victims of crime, defendants accused of crimes, consumers in debt, children in need of care or business people in commercial disputes. Our aim is to ensure that access is provided as quickly as possible and at lowest cost consistent with open justice, and that citizens have greater confidence in, and respect for, the system of justice.*

Courts deal with either or both of the two main divisions of legal work, criminal and civil. Criminal courts are where people who are accused of crimes either admit them or are tried and, if found guilty, have a penalty imposed. Civil courts are where people can seek remedies for injustices they think they have experienced. Family law, including divorce, adoption and child protection, is a part of civil law. Courts which make initial decisions – courts of first instance – should be distinguished from those which review the decisions of other courts – appeal courts. Some types of cases in which the legal issues may be similar, for example disputes about children or responsibility for accidents, are dealt with by one court rather than another because of their level of importance, or the amount of money at stake. However, these categories are not absolute, because some courts have both civil and criminal jurisdiction, and some courts make initial decisions and also hear appeals from other courts.

Courts have three primary roles, all of which reflect society's values in one form or another:

- to provide a fair and independent mechanism for upholding the values which society regards as important, which includes the means by which actions considered to be harmful or undesirable are discouraged and punished;

- to resolve disputes between people who are not able to resolve them independently; and

- to provide a safeguard against the abuse of power, in the form of impartial scrutiny of decisions and a means of redress if necessary.

The English court system is rather like a pyramid-shaped tree with a number of branches within it, supported by an extensive root structure. Essentially it is a bottom-heavy hierarchy, with magistrates' courts at the base, over which are Crown and County Courts, followed by the High Court, the Court of Appeal and, ultimately, the House of Lords (see Figure 2.1).

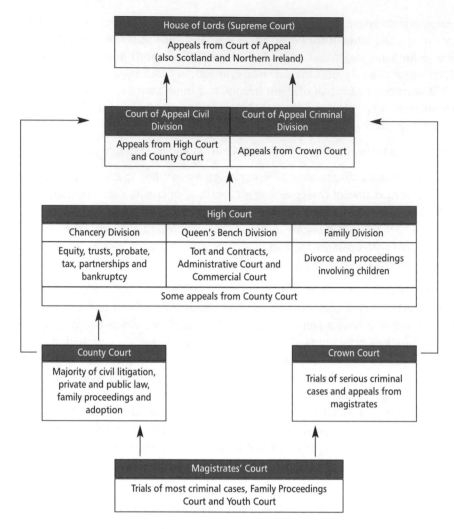

Figure 2.1 Outline of court structure in England and Wales

Magistrates' courts

For 650 years magistrates have undertaken the greater part of judicial work, and around 95 per cent of court business, comprising an annual caseload of more than four million, is conducted in 350 magistrates' courts in England and Wales. There are over 28,000 magistrates, evenly divided as to gender, with around 7 per cent from ethnic minority groups. Magistrates are unpaid, other than expenses, and do not need formal qualifications, though they do receive training. In addition to sitting in court, magistrates are expected to respond out of hours to urgent requests, such as warrants for arrest and search, or emergency protection orders, and to take declarations of various kinds.

Anyone can apply to be a magistrate, and you may have seen advertisements which encourage people to consider volunteering for the job. Local advisory committees make recommendations for appointment to the Lord Chancellor and applications are *welcomed from people from all walks of life who have the qualities and the time to serve as magistrates.* The age range for holding an appointment is 18–70, although anyone over 65 is unlikely to be newly appointed. In terms of gender, ethnic origin, geographic spread, occupation and political affiliation, each bench is required to broadly reflect the community it serves. However, perhaps not surprisingly, in view of the time commitment and the fact that it is an unpaid position, magistrates are likely to be middle-aged and middle-class people who are prominent in their local community through business, professional activities or charitable work. Usually magistrates sit in threes and for youth and family courts there must be a mix of genders.

Some magistrates' courts in London and larger cities, where there is a high volume of business, are presided over by district judges (magistrates' court), formerly known as stipendiary magistrates, who are full-time paid professional judges. There are also part-time deputy district judges (magistrates' court), barristers or solicitors in practice who are paid for sitting as judges. Because magistrates are not legally qualified, they have a qualified clerk to guide them on the law. Magistrates' courts deal with both criminal and some civil matters. In criminal cases, the magistrates' role is to decide on the facts of the case by assessing the evidence and to determine the sentence for anyone who is found guilty.

For criminal matters, magistrates' courts are divided into adult and youth courts, with the latter responsible for cases involving young people between the ages of 10 and 17. Youth courts are intended to be less formal than adult courts, both in relation to layout and the way in which proceedings are conducted, and hearings take place in private at a different time from adult court hearings. The press is normally allowed to attend, but the child or young person concerned must not be identified in any reports.

ACTIVITY 2.2

What do you think should be the age of criminal responsibility?

What possible consequences could result from it being 10, rather than 12, 14 or 16?

The age of criminal responsibility in England, 10, is one of the lowest in Europe, which means that many more young people here than in the rest of Europe have a criminal record by the time they become adult. A curious legal anomaly dating back to the Children and Young Persons Act 1933 means that in criminal courts 17-year-olds are regarded as adults, which has caused concern about their treatment in custody.

All criminal cases start, and most of them finish, in the magistrates' court. The few that do not are either so serious that magistrates' powers are considered insufficient to deal with them, or are offences for which the accused person has the right to ask for trial in the Crown Court in front of a judge and jury (known as *either-way offences*). Even if criminal cases are transferred to a higher court, magistrates still decide matters such as whether the accused person is to be released on bail while they wait and, if so, on what terms.

Magistrates' courts have a role in relation to some civil matters, such as licensing and council tax enforcement, and there is a family proceedings court, which deals with cases involving maintenance, domestic violence and the welfare of children.

Magistrates do not have robes and wear their ordinary clothes in court.

The Crown Court

For criminal cases, the Crown Court, of which there are 78 in England and Wales, is the next step up the court hierarchy. Crown Courts also hear appeals from magistrates' courts against conviction or sentence. The judge sits with two magistrates and the evidence is heard again, in effect a re-trial. There is, however, a risk for unsuccessful defendants in that Crown Courts have greater powers than magistrates and the sentence could be increased.

Judges in the Crown Court are usually full-time and salaried circuit judges, a title introduced when Crown Courts were established in 1971. However, the judicial system depends heavily on the assistance of part-time judges, known as recorders, most of whom are practising barristers or solicitors who sit as paid judges for three to six weeks each year. Anyone wishing to become a full-time judge normally first works as a part-time judge. The most serious cases in the Crown Court, such as murder, are usually tried by High Court judges, sometimes known as *red judges* on account of their red robes, who spend about half the legal year, around 18 weeks, sitting in Crown Courts around the country.

ACTIVITY 2.3

Crown Courts are open to the public, and observing a court in action is a good way of gaining an understanding of how they operate. If you explain to an usher why you are there, they should be able to direct you to a court where something interesting is going on. Take care not to enter or leave a court during the swearing in of the jury, or of a witness, or during the judge's summing up.

Family hearings are not open to the public, but many judges are willing to allow people with a professional interest to observe what happens in court as part of their training and development, so ask if arrangements can be made for you to visit a family court and perhaps have a meeting with the judge or magistrates.

County Courts

The 218 County Courts deal with almost all civil actions, within their prescribed financial and legal limits, such as unpaid debts, defective goods, personal injury, breach of contract or housing disputes. Remedies which can be awarded are usually either financial (damages) or restitutional (putting right whatever was complained of). County Courts also have an important role in relation to family matters, including divorce, domestic violence, adoption and local authority action to protect children. The latter types of case are normally heard in selected County Courts, designated as Care Centres, by judges who have received specialist training. As in Crown Courts, hearings can take place before circuit judges or recorders, but a considerable amount of County Court work is undertaken by district judges or part-time deputy district judges, who decide cases with a value less than £15,000, conduct consumer arbitrations and deal with preparations for trials and administrative arrangements.

In the past the law has had a reputation for not being particularly user-friendly. Recently, however, efforts have been made to introduce a more business-like culture, particularly in civil courts. County Court cases are allocated to one of three tracks, multi-track, fast track and small claims track, and are subject to ongoing case management until they come to trial or settlement is reached. To be allocated to the fast track, normally the amount at stake is between £5,000 and £15,000; it is anticipated that less than 30 weeks will be needed to prepare for the trial; and the hearing, if it happens, will not take longer than one day. Claims worth less than £5,000 are assigned to the small claims track, which does not require legal representation and is intended to be a simpler, more informal, way of resolving disputes. Claimants simply complete a form, many of which can be downloaded or completed online, and pay a fee in order to initiate an action. Money claim online is a similar service available to people seeking to recover money owed to them.

County Court hearings can be either private or public, although there is not usually much public interest in County Court business. Cases involving family matters and personal finances are usually heard in private, although in response to pressure, the government is considering making the operation of family courts more open and transparent.

ACTIVITY **2.4**

What factors can you identify for and against making family courts more open?

List the implications for all those with an interest in such proceedings (parents, children, lawyers, judges, professionals, the media, the government).

What factors do you think will influence the government's decision?

Not everyone is in favour of the proposals, and it has implications for social workers and other professionals who sometimes have to express opinions, or be associated with decisions, which may be deeply unpopular with one or more of the parties involved. However, the principles of transparency and openness are important in the context of fairness, and there has been a strong lobby from organisations such as Fathers for Justice which feels that the interests of users of family courts would be better served if the proceedings were open to public scrutiny.

Courts of first instance – family

Almost all courts of first instance have some family jurisdiction, and where a case is heard depends on its complexity. The lowest level of court which deals with family cases is a magistrates' family proceedings court. More complex cases are heard in County Courts by district or circuit judges, and the highest level of first-instance family court is the Family Division of the High Court.

The High Court

The next tier of court is the High Court which is divided into three divisions: Chancery, Queen's Bench and Family, each of which includes a Divisional Court and, in the Chancery and Queen's Bench Divisions, some specialist courts. There is considerable overlap between the work of the Chancery and Queen's Bench Divisions, but Queen's Bench deals with more important or higher value civil cases, such as personal injury, negligence, defamation and claims against local authorities for wrongful actions, and Chancery is concerned with matters such as trademarks and patents, bankruptcy, wills, financial regulation and disputes about trusts, land and leases. The Family Division, as its name suggests, hears more complex family law cases, including divorce, wardship, adoption, child abduction and public law proceedings under the Children Act 1989.

High Court trials take place before a High Court judge, a circuit judge sitting as a High Court judge, or a deputy High Court judge, usually a QC who is sitting as a part-time judge. Case management is undertaken, and many applications are dealt with, by junior judges, known in the Chancery and Queen's Bench Divisions as Masters and in the Family Division as Registrars.

Court of Appeal

Again, at this level there is a distinction between criminal and civil cases. The Criminal Division hears appeals against conviction or sentence, or both, from the Crown Court, and the Civil Division hears appeals in civil cases from the High Court and some appeals from County Courts.

House of Lords

As we have seen, the House of Lords will be replaced by a new Supreme Court in 2009.

Judicial review

This is the process by which a judge in the Administrative Court, a specialist court in the Queen's Bench Division, reviews the lawfulness of a decision or action taken by a public body. This can result in a declaration that the action concerned should be considered as having no effect (*quashing* the action), or a direction that something else be done. It is concerned with the decision-making process itself, rather than the conclusion which resulted, so a public body could make the same decision again, even if it was decided that the process leading to the first decision was unlawful. Cases come to the Administrative Court when an aggrieved person applies for permission to seek judicial review, which is granted if it appears that there is a case for investigation. At the subsequent hearing, lawyers for all parties affected can put forward arguments as to whether or not there has been a breach of the law.

There are several possible reasons why judicial review cases seem to attract so much attention. One is that there may be a number of different legal principles involved, and it may be unclear how they interact with each other, or which should prevail. For example, some applicants for judicial review have succeeded in suggesting that the provisions of the Human Rights Act 1998 should prevail over other rules. Another reason may be that people are now more inclined to challenge the actions of local or national government organisations. However, a significant factor, at least for local authorities, is that often there is insufficient time and resources to make decisions in accordance with all of the relevant law, and so inevitably they sometimes get it wrong.

European Courts

The Court of Justice of the European Union, often called the European Court, ensures that laws made by the European Union are interpreted and applied consistently in member states. Therefore, if an issue of European law arises, a court in a member state can refer it to the European Court, whose judgment must be applied by the original court when deciding the case. Such references are not often made from English courts, but those that are usually come from the House of Lords. When the European Convention on Human Rights was ratified by the UK in 1951, it was only binding on the government, not the courts. In 1965 the UK agreed to the citizen's right of direct petition to the European Court of Human Rights (ECtHR) in Strasbourg, and until the Convention was incorporated formally into domestic legislation by means of the Human Rights Act 1998, the UK lost more cases in the ECtHR than any other country. The purpose of the Human Rights Act was to permit alleged breaches of the Convention to be tried in English courts, to ensure that English courts take account of previous decisions of the ECtHR and to require all public authorities to act in accordance with the Convention's requirements. The ECtHR is not part of the court structure of England and Wales, and cases can only be heard there after passing through all appeal processes in the UK.

The judges

We have already seen that magistrates are unpaid and not legally qualified, and all other judges are legally qualified and paid, whether full- or part-time. Since April 2006, the Lord Chief Justice has been head of the judiciary in place of the Lord Chancellor.

The statistics relating to the age, gender and education of judges show that the majority of judges are white, male, middle-aged and middle-class, particularly in the higher courts. This partly reflects the training arrangements of the 1970s and 1980s, when it was difficult to qualify as a solicitor or barrister without independent financial support, and also the fact that working practices and career patterns at that time were not in any sense family-friendly. Of 108 High Court judges in post on 1 April 2006, only eleven were female, of whom seven had appointed in the previous five years. Three out of 37 Appeal Court judges, and one of the 12 Law Lords, were female. One High Court judge and ten out of 631 circuit judges were from an ethnic minority background. Most judges on appointment are at least in their mid-forties and have practised as barristers. No High Court judge in post on 1 April 2006 was appointed younger than 45, and more than half were between 49 and 55. The oldest serving High Court judge was 71 and the youngest 47. As you would expect, the age profile of Court of Appeal judges is older still, with all the judges aged between 54 and 69. The youngest Law Lord was 60 and the oldest 72. The retiring age for judges is 70, but those appointed before it was reduced from 72 are entitled to remain in post until that age.

Measures have recently been introduced to increase diversity among the judiciary. Circuit judges and below can apply to sit part-time, and career breaks of between three months and three years are available. There is a work shadowing scheme for those who are interested in applying, a DVD entitled *A Day in the Life of a Judge* has been produced and a dedicated website aims to make judges appear less remote. It remains to be seen what effect these have on recruitment and public perception.

How are judges appointed?

High Court judges, circuit judges, recorders and district judges are appointed by the Queen on the recommendation of the Lord Chancellor, and deputy district judges are appointed by the Lord Chancellor. Until recently, High Court judges did not apply for the post but informal approaches were made to potential candidates by the Lord Chancellor's officials. Anyone wishing to become a district judge, recorder or circuit judge has always had to apply for the post and this now also applies to High Court judges, with the process managed by the Judicial Appointments Commission. Many serving judges were appointed under the previous ad hoc system, which clearly lacked the transparency you would expect in relation to such important appointments, but there has already been some disquiet expressed about apparent irregularities in the shortlisting procedures operated by the Judicial Appointments Commission (*Daily Telegraph*, 22 February 2007). Appeal Court judges are appointed by the Queen on the recommendation of the Prime Minister and there is no competitive selection process as the pool of potential candidates is essentially only High Court judges.

Who are the lawyers?

If you are legally represented in court, the person who speaks for you will be either a solicitor or barrister and, depending on the type and complexity of the case, there may be a legal team of several members. Most barristers and solicitors have studied law at university, and all have completed vocational training in the practical aspects of their role. Aspiring solicitors and barristers used to have to pay for the vocational stage of their training, which clearly limited access to the profession, but it is now usual for training salaries to be paid. Lawyers also have to undergo continuing professional development, the requirements of which are greatest in the first years of practice. Interestingly, these are less than the GSCC requirements of 15 days or 90 hours over three years to maintain registration as a social worker.

Barristers are known collectively as *the Bar*. This comes from the physical layout of the Inns of Court where there used to be a rail dividing student barristers from the governors of the Inn, the Benchers, and students were *called to the Bar* to be admitted as barristers. Individual barristers are sometimes referred to as *counsel*, as in *Queen's Counsel*, which simply means someone who gives advice. Barristers are either junior barristers or Queen's Counsel. The designation QC indicates that a barrister is recognised as experienced and knowledgeable in a particular field (*learned in the law*), rather like a medical consultant, not that they actually advise the queen or the government. They are also sometimes known as *leading counsel*. Most QCs are appointed around the age of 40, and have been in practice for at least 15 years. Since 2004, the process of appointment has involved the assessment of applicants by a firm of recruitment consultants and, inevitably, the payment of a substantial fee, whether or not the application is successful.

Traditionally, solicitors give general legal advice and prepare cases for trial by assembling documents and interviewing potential witnesses, while barristers give specialist legal advice and present cases in court. However, this distinction can be misleading as some solicitors now present cases in court as solicitor advocates and are highly specialist in their field. If both a solicitor and barrister are involved in a case, in court the solicitor supplies documents and information to the barrister and takes notes, particularly while the barrister is questioning a witness or speaking. In complex cases, a QC may be engaged, supported by a junior barrister, and they share the task of assessing the papers, preparing the arguments to be put to the court and, usually, the questioning of witnesses and note-taking at the hearing.

Most solicitors practise as partners in, or employees of, a firm, or as members, or employees, of a limited liability partnership. Some organisations, such as large companies and local authorities, employ their own solicitors. Barristers can be employed directly, but most are in private practice as sole practitioners, without partners in the business sense. Barristers' *chambers* are a set of offices, membership of which enables them to share business expenses, but not fees, with other barristers. Most chambers have business managers, called clerks, who obtain work for the barristers and negotiate fees. Historically, chambers had to be in one of the four Inns of Court in London, but now there are barristers' chambers in towns and cities throughout the country.

Crown Prosecution Service

The CPS, headed by the Director of Public Prosecutions and staffed by lawyers, decides whether a person should be prosecuted in court, based on the evidence gathered during a police investigation and whether the prosecution is in the public interest. The police can make prosecution decisions in relation to most road traffic offences and some public order offences.

Legal Services Commission

This agency, which incorporates the Criminal Defence Service and Community Legal Service, manages requests for legal representation at public expense. In Chapter 13 we consider how recent developments in the public funding of legal services are affecting people who are involved in, or wish to initiate, legal proceedings.

How are cases decided in court?

There are two basic approaches.

- **The adversarial approach** has historically been adopted in England and Wales. In this the court relies on each party to put forward rival arguments between which it can decide. The theory is that if it is up to the parties to try and persuade the court of the rightness of their respective positions, they will do everything possible to achieve that, and so all the relevant evidence and argument will be put before the court.

- **The inquisitorial approach** is one in which the court reaches a decision based on the outcome of its own inquiries. Many people feel that this approach, which is common in European courts, is more suitable in civil proceedings, particularly family cases.

Alternative dispute resolution

In cases in which society has an interest, it not usually appropriate to try to reach an agreement to resolve the issue. If someone is accused of a crime for which they will be punished if guilty and they deny the offence, the scope for compromise is limited. However, in disputes over money or property, the parties may be able to reach an acceptable agreement. This is a rationale behind changes in the conduct of civil litigation, given effect by the Civil Procedure Rules 1999, which emphasise the courts' role in assisting parties to civil actions to compromise their dispute. The methods available include the following:

- **Mediation** The court cannot itself, through judges, mediate and guide parties to a settlement because, if agreement is not reached, the court has to decide the dispute and its impartiality could be compromised if it had previously expressed a view on the merits of the case. In addition to pre-trial discussions between the respective lawyers, courts therefore encourage the involvement of another party to help reach a settlement, which has led to the development of the role of professional mediator. As they expect to be paid, mediators tend to be engaged when quite a lot of money is at stake and the potential costs of a full hearing are high, but some courts operate voluntary, free mediation schemes, and mediation is widely used in family cases, such as disputes over contact, or financial arrangements after a divorce.

- **Adjudication** This is a process in which a quicker, if less thorough, assessment is made of a case than would happen if it was heard to the bitter end in court.

- **Arbitration** This is best suited to cases which involve the quality of goods or work. If someone buys a second-hand car and complains about its condition, a person who is knowledgeable about second-hand cars could be appointed as arbitrator and, after examining the car, offer an independent view as to whether the alleged defect was to be expected in a car of the age and type in question.

Research Summary

Mantle's (2001) investigation into the effectiveness of family mediation services involved a survey of parents who had reached agreement during mediation, with particular attention paid to the experience of fathers. The parts played by mediators, lawyers and judges are explored through the eyes of the parents, and the traditional assumption that court-based interventions are less likely to be successful is challenged.

A major motivation behind the reforms introduced by the Civil Procedure Rules was the desire to reduce the costs of litigation, which is a theme we revisit when we look at representation in court. The reforms have led to a significant reduction in the volume of civil litigation, which means that cases reach trial stage much more quickly than previously. About 95 per cent of civil actions are still settled before trial. The scope for compromise in family disputes, particularly those involving children, is more limited than in disputes about money or property. However, even then, the emphasis is on achieving a resolution which minimises damaging confrontation and enables the parties to work together in the future. Consequently, judges feel able to participate more actively in family cases than in other types of case.

Children and Family Court Advisory and Support Service (CAFCASS)

The Children and Family Court Advisory and Support Service (CAFCASS) is an independent public agency set up in 2001, which brought together the Family Court Welfare Service, the Guardian ad Litem services and the Children's Division of the Official Solicitor, and is responsible for working with, and preparing reports in respect of, children involved in family court proceedings. In private law, its work is increasingly focused on reducing conflict and helping parents reach agreement. In public law, over half its caseload relates to representing children in care proceedings, with the remainder involving adoption, emergency protection orders and applications to discharge care orders.

The future

The court system in England and Wales is not very logical and is largely the product of the historical developments outlined in Chapter 1. In practice, there are fairly sharp distinctions between criminal law, family law and the rest of civil law. It therefore seems sensible to have separate criminal courts and judges, and the government is considering changes in civil and family courts of first instance, so that all cases would be heard in one type of court (DCA, 2005).

In relation to crime, the government is extending the experimental community courts set up in Liverpool and Salford, with the aim of providing speedy handling of cases, reparation of harm, reintegration of offenders and the building up of communities. Launching the new courts in November 2006, Lord Falconer, the Lord Chancellor, said: *We need to do justice differently. Communities affected by crime want to see justice done in ways that connect more closely to the community* (*Daily Telegraph*, 23 November 2006).

The Mental Capacity Act 2005 provides for a new Court of Protection which will have wide-ranging jurisdiction in relation to the determination of capacity and 'best interests' decisions concerning the health, welfare, finances and property of people who have been assessed as lacking capacity to manage all or some of their own affairs.

C H A P T E R S U M M A R Y

This chapter describes the legal system as it is today, to be read against the historical background outlined in the previous chapter. Having enjoyed a fairly settled period during the second half of the twentieth century, the law is now experiencing a pace of change which will be familiar to social workers. As we will find in the next chapter, in some respects, such as regulation, accountability and service user involvement, social work is ahead of the law, and as much as anything this will enable you to express a view on the way in which the legal profession is developing.

FURTHER READING

There are numerous books on the English legal system. An accessible general text is:

Partington, M. (2006) *Introduction to the English Legal System*, 3rd edn. Oxford: Oxford University Press.

WEBSITES

www.cafcass.gov.uk
Children and Family Court Advisory and Support Service – its annual report gives an overview of changes within the family court system and examples of innovative practice.

www.hmcourts-service.gov.uk
The HMCS website has a wide range of information for users of courts.

www.judiciary.gov.uk
A website managed by the Judicial Communications Office, which aims to make the judiciary more accessible.

www.magistrates-association.org.uk
Includes an interactive youth site.

Chapter 3

Values and principles in law and social work

Introduction

If only social workers would realise we are human. We have problems. We have piles. We really want to know, as human to human, what they think. (Family court judge)

Social workers often regard lawyers as remote and detached from real life, and we acknowledge that some of them still seem to cultivate this image. However, in our experience it is much less common than it used to be. The legal profession, like any other, incorporates a wide range of skills, personal characteristics and beliefs in its practitioners and, like social work, has experienced fairly dramatic changes in recent years. These include training costs and requirements, regulation and accountability, restrictions in the public funding of legal services and media attention. One of the aims of this book is to demystify aspects of the law which create barriers for social workers doing court work, and key aspects of the interface between them are the values and principles which shape the two professions.

In this chapter we show that how lawyers are governed, and the principles which underpin their profession, are similar to those which apply to social work. There are issues which apply to lawyers, and not to social workers, because of the nature of their work, and there are issues which apply to solicitors, but not to barristers, because of their different roles. However, principles such as fairness, honesty, transparency, confidentiality, anti-discriminatory practice and commitment to social justice are as central to the law as they are to social work, and there have been recent examples of judges and lawyers resisting what they regard as attacks by politicians on the essential values of their profession.

Where there are perceived barriers between individual members of each profession, we suggest that in part this may stem from the contrasting skills and approaches which lawyers and social workers bring to problem-solving and from differences in personal attributes and motivation towards their respective careers.

ACTIVITY **3.1**

- *Without thinking too deeply, list ten words which you might use to describe lawyers.*

- *Next, list ten words to describe another professional, such as a teacher or doctor.*

- *Now assess whether the words you have chosen are generally positive, neutral, negative, or a mixture of the three.*

- *What does this tell you about your preconceived ideas about the legal profession?*

This exercise will demonstrate that we all hold preconceptions about people whom we perceive as different from ourselves. Sometimes these attitudes stem from experience, but others may be based on unchecked assumptions, inaccurate information or unconscious prejudices. It is only by acknowledging this possibility and addressing the consequences that we can begin to identify and find ways of overcoming the barriers which impede effective professional relationships.

A statutory professional framework

Social workers

Until the Care Standards Act 2000, social work as a profession was not regulated by statute. There was no restriction on anyone calling themselves a social worker and there were no rules or statutory professional body to regulate standards, although some social workers voluntarily belonged to the British Association of Social Workers which required them to adhere to its codes of practice. In general, however, the public – and service users in particular – had no guidance on what to expect from social workers and no means of redress if they were dissatisfied or poorly served. The General Social Care Council (GSCC) has now taken on this role, but it will inevitably take time for its influence to be felt by users of social work services and for it to convince those who have tended to be critical that social work has earned the right to be regarded as a profession. The GSCC is currently ahead of the Bar Council and Law Society in that the majority of its council members, who determine issues concerning professional standards, are lay people rather than members of the social care profession. However, both lawyers' organisations are now moving away from regulation exclusively by members of their profession.

Barristers

In the Middle Ages most skilled workers belonged to a guild which maintained standards and regulated its members. As we have seen, barristers' guilds were the Inns of Court, and these arrangements continued until 1894, when the General Council of the Bar, generally called the Bar Council, was established to determine questions of professional etiquette. The Bar Council also has a statutory role in relation to barristers as a result of the Courts and Legal Services Act 1990 which provides that a person only has a right to appear in a court for a party, *a right of audience*, if they comply with the Act's requirements. Among other things, barristers must be educated and trained to approved standards, they must be members of a professional body with enforceable rules of conduct and they must provide a proper professional service, which is similar to the requirements of other professions, including social work.

Solicitors

In this book, we are only concerned with solicitors conducting litigation, not with other services which they provide, such as conveyancing. The Law Society of England and Wales, usually called the Law Society, was formed in 1845, with the purpose of *promoting professional improvement and facilitating the acquisition of legal knowledge*. It evolved into providing the regulation of solicitors, but at that time the Master of the Rolls was responsible for the supervision of solicitors. The *Rolls* are the rolls on which solicitors' names are entered when they are admitted as solicitors. The Master of the Rolls is now the senior judge of the Civil Division of the Court of Appeal and still retains functions over solicitors. Because solicitors are more numerous than barristers, and because they have more opportunity than barristers to commit misdeeds due to their access to clients' money, Parliament passed laws affecting the conduct of solicitors rather earlier than in the case of barristers. The principal Act is the Solicitors Act 1974, although it has been altered considerably since it was first passed. Solicitors cannot practise unless they have been admitted as a solicitor, their name is on the roll of solicitors (that is, they have not been struck off) and they hold a practising certificate, which can have conditions attached. The cost of a practising certificate is much greater than that required by the GSCC for registration, but the GSCC goes further than the Law Society in making inquiries about the health of applicants for registration and requiring applications to be verified and endorsed by an approved person.

Professional standards

Like most professionals, lawyers take their professional standing seriously. For example, barristers do not handle clients' money, an important distinction between them and solicitors and one of the fundamental principles set out in the barristers' code of conduct. In addition to honesty and the duty to ensure that their conduct is not prejudicial to the administration of justice, or likely to diminish public confidence in the legal profession, barristers operate under other strongly worded principles in their code of conduct, which may partly explain the single-minded way in which they sometimes appear to approach their work:

303 A barrister:

(a) *must promote and protect fearlessly, and by all proper and lawful means, the lay client's best interests, and do so without regard to his own interests or to any consequences to himself or any other person (including any professional client or own intermediary or another barrister);*

(b) *owes his primary duty as between the lay client and any professional client or other intermediary to the lay client and must not permit the intermediary to limit his discretion as to how the interests of the lay client can best be served;...*

307 A barrister must not:

(a) *permit his absolute independence, integrity and freedom from external pressures to be compromised;*

(b) *do anything in such circumstances as may lead to any inference that his independence may be compromised;*

(c) *compromise his professional standards in order to please his client, the court or a third party.*

Although these principles, of which we only provide an extract, are similar to those of social work, there is an edge to the language which makes them, if anything, more demanding than those of social work, which tend to use more qualified expressions such as *seek to ensure* and *as far as possible*. However, employed social workers usually have interests and duties other than those owed to their clients, which presents them with dilemmas which lawyers may sometimes fail to appreciate.

Barristers' professional standards are mirrored by the solicitors' rules, of which there is a huge number covering a wide range of issues. The most fundamental are the Solicitors' Practice Rules 1990, the most basic of which is Rule 1, in which again the client's needs are central:

A solicitor shall not do anything in the course of practice which compromises or impairs, or is likely to compromise or impair, the solicitor's independence or integrity, and duty to act in the best interests of the client.

Solicitor advocates are also bound by the Law Society's code of advocacy, which mostly reproduces the principles of the code of conduct of the Bar. In 2007 the Law Society was restructured and established a separate arm, the Solicitors Regulation Authority, which includes lay representation and an independent Consumer Complaints Board.

ACTIVITY 3.2

In relation to professional standards, if you were in the position of a client, would you regard the following behaviours as more serious or more likely in a social worker or a lawyer?

- *Spending more time on cases they find rewarding.*

- *Offering unrealistic assurances.*

- *Sharing personal experiences.*

- *Not preparing adequately for decision-making meetings.*

- *Being influenced by people they perceive as more powerful.*

- *Avoiding clients they find difficult.*

- *Ignoring clients' wishes and instructions.*

- *Giving advice beyond the limits of their expertise.*

- *Not keeping the client fully informed.*

- *Blaming policies, procedures or lack of resources for any shortfall in services.*

In encouraging you to think about clients' expectations of lawyers and social workers, and the pressures and priorities of each profession, this exercise will help you recognise similarities and differences in the ways in which lawyers and social workers approach their work.

Principle of being non-judgmental

This principle is fundamental to social work; however, bearing in mind the fact that *judging* people is a central task of courts, how can it be said that lawyers are non-judgmental? Over the years, some stories have circulated to illustrate the sort of professional dilemmas which lawyers may face:

A barrister successfully defended a man against a charge of burglary, in which it was alleged that he had stolen a valuable gold watch. After he was acquitted, he leant over the dock towards his barrister, saying in a loud stage whisper, 'So, what shall I do with the watch?'

In another case it was reported that a man who had been acquitted of stealing antique jewellery sent his solicitor a letter of thanks, enclosing a gift of Victorian silver cufflinks.

These rather unlikely stories nevertheless raise an issue which is sometimes put to lawyers on social occasions: how can they defend someone they know to be guilty, or present a case they know, or suspect, to be false? The answer is not dissimilar to the one that social workers might give if asked how they could work with people who had neglected or abused children. Lawyers' professional duty is to do their best for their client, which involves giving the best advice and trying to achieve the best outcome in any legal proceedings. It does not matter whether lawyers believe their clients or not; it is their responsibility to advise on the risks of a court not accepting what they say. If a client persists in presenting a particular account, despite being advised of the possible consequences, the lawyer's duty is to present the case in the best way possible, without deceiving or misleading the court (see under Fairness below). If, unusually, a client tells their lawyer that they are guilty but nevertheless intend to fight the case to the bitter end, or that the evidence they intend to give is untrue, the lawyer would be unable to act for them.

The principles which underpin this approach are as follows:

- Lawyers should not judge their clients and must proceed on the basis that what they say is true, however unlikely it may seem.

- Even people who are dishonest or guilty of crimes have a right to legal advice and representation.

- The rules of English criminal law allow technical points to be used for the benefit of defendants which can, of course, result in a guilty person being acquitted. Lawyers who take advantage of technical points on their clients' behalf are simply carrying out their professional duty by following the rules.

Confidentiality

Confidentiality is so fundamental to how lawyers operate that you have to look quite hard in their codes of conduct to find any reference to it. Without confidentiality, the administration of justice could not work, which is explained in more detail in the next chapter. Barristers and solicitors are bound to keep confidential the affairs of their clients but, as with social workers, this confidentiality is not absolute. In limited circumstances it is permissible, or even required, for lawyers to divulge information obtained in confidence from their clients. The most obvious examples are where disclosure is required by law, such as in cases involving money laundering, drug trafficking or terrorism, and when lawyers must also comply with any order to produce documents required by the police under the Police and Criminal Evidence Act 1984.

Lawyers also have a duty to the court to assist in the administration of justice and not to deceive or mislead. So, if a court requires a lawyer to disclose confidential information, they must comply. This is rare but it could happen, for example in order to discover the whereabouts of a child.

More difficult is the situation in which a lawyer, while not being required to, may wish to disclose information from a client which may affect another person. If someone tells their lawyer that they intend to commit a crime like kidnap a child, the law treats the information as not being confidential and so it can be disclosed. If there is no suggestion of a potential crime, the lawyer's position is difficult. In principle, any information provided by a client should be kept confidential. However, professionals can disclose confidential information in exceptional circumstances.

CASE EXAMPLE

W v. Edgell [1990] 1 All ER 835

After shooting several people, W was detained in a secure psychiatric hospital. Subsequently he applied to a Mental Health Review Tribunal to be discharged, and while his responsible medical officer supported the application, the Secretary of State opposed it. W's solicitors asked Dr Edgell, a consultant psychiatrist, to prepare a report which it was hoped would support W's application for release. However, Dr Edgell concluded that W had a psychopathic disorder, combined with a long-standing interest in firearms and explosives, which made him a continuing risk to the public. When Dr Edgell's report was received by W's solicitors, W withdrew his application and the report would not normally have been disclosed to anyone else. When Dr Edgell discovered this, he sent a copy to the hospital, which sent it to the Secretary of State, who sent it to the Mental Health Review Tribunal. W then sued Dr Edgell for breach of confidence, but his claim failed on the ground that the public interest in disclosing Dr Edgell's professional opinion was greater than the public interest in maintaining W's confidentiality.

In this case it was a question of balance, which is why it is difficult to say how great the public interest in disclosure needs to be in order to override the principle of confidentiality. All you can say is that for a lawyer it would need to be a very important interest to override the confidentiality which is fundamental between lawyers and clients.

In the case of other professionals, the position is less clear. An ordinary employee, with no particular duties of confidentiality other than not to disclose the private business of the employer, is free to disclose any significant breach of the law by his employer. However, most professionals, including social workers, operate on the basis that confidentiality is integral to their work, and most professional rules or codes of practice support this principle. Therefore a failure to maintain confidentiality could expose a professional to disciplinary action by their employer or professional body. No disciplinary tribunal would criticise a professional who was required by a court to disclose confidential information. As in the Edgell case, courts always aim to balance the public interest in knowing the information with the interest of the professional's client in keeping it private. However, historically courts have tended to insist that non-legal professionals do disclose confidential information, if it is thought that there is a valid reason for its disclosure. A journalist, for example, cannot refuse to disclose his sources. A probation officer is not entitled to keep information from a court, nor are an accountant, a banker or a doctor. There is, however, an exception in relation to information which non-lawyers obtain in the course of trying to negotiate the settlement of a dispute. Discussions in these circumstances are treated by the law as *without prejudice*, which means that everything which is revealed is privileged, no matter who was involved and whatever the outcome, even if the person concerned poked his nose into the dispute without asking. For example, as long as he is acting as a conciliator, confidential information received by a probation officer is privileged and does not have to be revealed to the court. We consider without prejudice communications further in Chapter 5.

Conflict of interest

It probably goes without saying that barristers and solicitors are not permitted to become involved in conflicts of interest. For barristers, two types of conflict are contemplated by their code of conduct.

- They must not accept instructions if, as a result, they would be professionally embarrassed, which includes lacking sufficient experience or competence to handle the case or not having the time to prepare it properly. We are sure that social workers would welcome a similar professional rule. A connection with someone such as the client or a court, which makes it difficult to remain or be seen to be objective, or a risk of conflict between two or more clients or of confidential information being leaked between clients, are also included.

- As barristers are usually instructed by solicitors, there is a particular problem if a barrister decides that their instructing solicitor has been negligent in advice given to the client or in the conduct of the case. However, it could also be a less extreme situation where there is no suggestion of negligence, but the barrister thinks that the client would be better off instructing another solicitor. If a barrister thinks that there is a conflict between the client and the instructing solicitor, he must tell the client to go elsewhere. There is a specific rule about this because a barrister who does this is likely not to receive any more work from the solicitor who instructed him, which could be a powerful incentive to keep quiet.

The solicitors' rule against conflict of interest is more straightforward. There is a duty not to act if the solicitor, or his practice, owes separate duties to two or more clients in relation to the same matter or if the duty to the client conflicts with the solicitor's own interests. However, solicitors can act for two or more clients in the same matter if they have a common interest in it and all the parties agree. This might happen, for example, in a child case where a solicitor could act for both parents.

ACTIVITY 3.3

List some potential conflicts of interest that a social worker may encounter (for example, receiving a referral which relates to a family known to you personally). Now, assess how far the GSCC Codes of Practice help to guide or protect you in these situations.

This exercise encourages you to consider further the similarities and differences between lawyers and social workers, particularly in relation to the level of protection or support each can expect from their codes of practice.

Fairness

An aspect which concerns many people when dealing with lawyers is how they treat you in court, in particular when cross-examining you. You should be reassured that it is not open season on witnesses for barristers or solicitor advocates, and their rules clearly state what they can or cannot do. In particular, each:

- *must not make statements or ask questions which are merely scandalous, or intended or calculated only to vilify, insult or annoy either a witness or some other person;*

- *must if possible avoid the naming in open court of third parties whose character would thereby be impugned;*

- *must not by assertion in a speech impugn a witness whom he has had an opportunity to cross-examine unless in cross-examination he has given the witness an opportunity to answer the allegation;*

- *must not suggest that a victim, witness or other person is guilty of crime, fraud or misconduct or make any defamatory aspersion on the conduct of any other person or attribute to another person the crime or conduct of which his lay client is accused unless such allegations go to a matter in issue (including the credibility of the witness) which is material to the lay client's case and appear to him to be supported by reasonable grounds.*

(CCB Rule 708; Law Society's Code of Advocacy Rule 7.1)

This means that you should only be cross-examined on the facts of the case, your credibility or your competence. You should not be criticised, unless it is relevant to the case and you have been given an opportunity to answer any criticism.

There are other aspects of fairness which are important in the context of understanding what happens in court. Barristers are not allowed to put forward an argument in court unless they consider that it is properly arguable. They cannot, therefore, just put forward any argument suggested by their client. Barristers and solicitor advocates must bring the court's attention to all relevant decisions, including those which do not support their client's case, and if something goes wrong or there is an irregularity, they cannot keep it quiet in the hope of an appeal but must bring it to the court's attention. They also must not make up the evidence.

More generally, solicitors must not behave deceitfully or so as to take an unfair advantage of anyone. Therefore you ought to be able to have confidence in their frankness and honesty. Once in court, you are unlikely to have contact with solicitors for an opposite party, because they are not supposed to interview any client who has retained their own solicitor, which, as a social worker involved in court proceedings, is likely to include you. In dealing with legal representatives for opposing parties, solicitors have a duty to behave with frankness and good faith, consistent with their duty to their clients. While solicitors may not feel able to disclose confidential information relating to their client, they must certainly not mislead.

The issue of fairness in relation to social workers is explored in more detail in Chapter 7. However, those who have contributed to this book have emphasised its importance in court settings.

> *Clients get very upset if facts are not presented fairly, even if they relate to something which seems quite unimportant. Once that happens, mistrust develops, which extends into more important areas, and is very difficult to overcome.* (Independent advocate)

Anti-discriminatory practice

The strongest framework of anti-discriminatory practice relates to barristers, who must not discriminate directly or indirectly on grounds of race, colour, ethnic or national origin, nationality, citizenship, sex, sexual orientation, marital status or political persuasion. Solicitors seem to be a little less constrained by what is prohibited, but through their rules both professions demonstrate a strong commitment to the promotion and maintenance of equality.

Partnership

From the start of their training, social workers are encouraged to see partnership with clients as the foundation of ethical practice, which is one reason why they feel uneasy in legal settings, where rules can appear to take precedence over clients' wishes and feelings. Lawyers' relationships with their clients start by receiving instructions. They then advise them and, whether or not the advice is accepted, try to obtain the result closest to what their client wants, which is a form of partnership. However, the partnership is subject to market forces, in that if the client is not satisfied, they can usually go elsewhere. For social workers partnership has additional dimensions, and involves a delicate balancing act between maximising choice for their clients, and carrying out legal powers and duties, while taking account of the resources available. Also, social workers have to work with involuntary clients, which lawyers, for the most part, do not.

How lawyers approach problems

In order to work effectively in legal settings, it is not necessary for you to learn to think like a lawyer. However, you do need to engage with the complexity of the law–practice interface (Cull and Roche, 2001), which is easier if you understand how lawyers think.

Through their training, lawyers learn how to interpret the law and apply it to solving legal problems. As we have seen, their first involvement in a case is likely to involve being asked for advice. In order to be able to consider what legal principles may apply in any situation, they have to assemble and evaluate material which shows the facts, or what a court, if the matter is contentious, might find that the facts are. They should know what types of facts might be relevant to their advice and, as we have seen, they do not need to be satisfied that everything they are told by their client is true. However, they need to see all relevant documents and any other evidence which supports the client's case, so that they can assess how a court might decide the case if there is a challenge and advise accordingly. Once the client's version of events has been established, it is possible to apply the law to it, which involves considering any relevant statutes or regulations and any relevant cases which have been decided previously. It is the focus on the law, rather than any other approach to the facts, which distinguishes the lawyer's approach from that of a non-lawyer.

CASE EXAMPLE

Birmingham City Council v. H (No. 3) [1994] 2 WLR 31

This case involved a baby with a 15-year-old mother, who was herself looked after by the local authority and had complex needs. A social worker would regard them both as equally entitled to services, but the legal approach was different. The House of Lords put the welfare of the baby as being paramount above that of the mother, because the court was dealing with an application concerning the baby, not the mother.

This example illustrates the fact that whatever non-lawyers might think are the ethical rights or wrongs of a case, or whatever they consider would be a desirable result, lawyers are concerned primarily with what the client's instructions are, and what, if any, legal duties and powers are applicable to a particular situation. Once a case comes to court, rather than objectively to seek justice or establish the truth, the lawyer's aim is to obtain the most satisfactory outcome for their client, consistent with their own professional rules and their duty to the court, which involves deciding, in consultation with their client, how best to present the case without misleading the court. We explore in Chapter 5 the relevance of court rules, but in many instances it is possible to compare the lawyer's preparation of a case with preparing a game plan. For example, if a potential witness is known to be frail and likely to become confused, it might be decided not to call them to give evidence to avoid risking the case being harmed by the witness creating a poor impression. Court hearings are, of course, not a game in the normal sense, but they are about making decisions in accordance with the law, which could be said to represent the rules of a game. Whoever wins is decided by applying the rules to the circumstances of the case. The only mechanism which exists for finding out what really happened in any situation is a public inquiry, which is very rarely established.

Motivation and personal attributes

I don't think I've ever met a lawyer who didn't appear supremely confident. (Expert witness)

When considering the nature of the relationships between social workers and lawyers, it is worth reflecting on your motivation for taking up a social work career and what is it about social work that appeals to you. You may have been influenced by a family member, or by personal experience of giving or receiving help; you may feel that you can identify with people who are socially disadvantaged or excluded; you may hope that working with people will bring particular challenges and rewards; you may have been told by others that you are a good listener; or you may have enjoyed supporting people with various difficulties in the past. If you ask lawyers why they chose the legal profession, they are likely to offer very different reasons, such as an interest in researching academic aspects of the law, an attraction to the drama, or even glamour, of the courtroom and the possibility of earning a reasonable amount of money. The contrast between these motivating factors goes some way towards explaining how tensions can develop between the two professions.

Most of the lawyers you meet professionally will be experienced and comfortable in court, which requires high levels of personal and professional confidence. However, for social workers, such perceived levels of confidence can sit uneasily with their training and commitment to identify and minimise power differentials and communication barriers between themselves and service users.

CHAPTER SUMMARY

In this chapter we have explored the values and principles which may be common to law and social work, and also potential areas of tension. The key to effective inter-professional working is an understanding of each person's position, which involves being proactive in exploring similarities and differences. We suggest that concern about perceived differences between the two professions often prevents social workers from taking advantage of the opportunities presented by the many common themes contained within their respective values, principles and professional codes.

FURTHER READING

Beckett, C. and Maynard, A. (2005) *Values and Ethics in Social Work*. London: Sage.
This text includes some relevant exercises and comparative analysis of the professional standards and regulation of social work and law.

WEBSITES

www.barcouncil.org.uk
The Bar Council.

gscc.org.uk
The General Social Care Council.

lawsociety.org.uk
The Law Society.

Chapter 4
Legal language and concepts

Introduction

Over nine out of ten cases heard by the Court of Appeal or the House of Lords either turn upon or involve the meaning of words. (Lord Hailsham, former Lord Chancellor, Hamlyn Lecture, 1983)

Lawyers thrive on words, as anyone who has ever read a legal document or communicated with lawyers can testify. Like most professionals, lawyers are also attracted to jargon, and a further barrier to communication in legal contexts is that Latin, Norman French and other historical expressions are still used, together with complex vocabulary and sentence construction. However, efforts are being made to introduce more accessible language into legislation and many Latin expressions have been replaced by English versions in order to make legal processes more easily understood.

In this chapter we try to demystify some of the expressions and concepts which are used by lawyers so that you can better understand what is going on. We do not define every legal term which exists, but we explain those which you are most likely to meet.

Types of law

Civil law

Confusingly, this expression has different meanings depending upon the context. In England and Wales, it usually means the law which applies to citizens when dealing between themselves, rather than the law which regulates the behaviour of members of society, which is the criminal law. However, sometimes civil law is used in distinction from common law, which we explained in the first chapter. The concept of civil law is derived in theory from Roman law, which means that the laws are written down in codes as, for example, in France. In broad terms, common law countries are England and Wales, Ireland, Commonwealth countries and the United States of America. Civil law countries are Scotland, all European countries and most other countries other than Commonwealth countries and the United States of America. Perhaps surprisingly, most Islamic countries are civil law countries with codes of law and do not primarily depend on Shariah law based on the Koran.

Common law

We have seen common law contrasted with civil law and we have explained its meaning in other contexts in the first chapter.

Criminal law

This is the law which every citizen must obey. Although it is possible for private individuals to prosecute people for breaching the criminal law, its main feature is that it is society, in the form of the state, which tries to ensure that the criminal law is obeyed and that those who break it are punished. Today most prosecutions are undertaken by the Crown Prosecution Service. However, in the Crown Court the name of the case against an accused person is always *R v.*, in which *R* represents Latin for *Regina* meaning Queen, or *Rex* meaning King. The v., which appears in all titles of legal cases, means *versus*, which is Latin for *against*. The Queen prosecutes people in the Crown Court on behalf of society, because historically it was the Crown's role to protect citizens against criminals.

Sources of law

Common law and equity

We have already explained that one of the meanings of common law is the law which has developed as a result of decisions of judges and that the rules of equity developed to supplement the common law. One of the remedies which equity invented was the injunction.

Precedent

A precedent is a decision in a case in which legal reasoning has been established. Precedent without an *a* describes the system by which judges must take account of previous decisions where relevant legal reasoning has been decided. First, they have to decide whether there is a relevant precedent which should be applied to the case. If there is, and the decision is from a court higher than the court hearing the case, it must be followed. Judges are not bound to follow decisions from lower courts or those on the same level, but may do so.

Statute

This is law which has been passed by Parliament or the Commission of the European Union, either by means of Acts or Statutory Instruments, the latter of which are made by government ministers, subject to approval by Parliament. Statutory Instruments are called something like *Regulations* or *Rules* or an *Order* and are identified by a number and the year in which they were passed. European Union laws which apply in England and Wales are either Regulations or Directives and again are identified by a number and the year in which they were passed. Only Regulations have direct effect as soon as they have been made. Directives require our Parliament to make a law to bring into effect the relevant European Union law.

Common law, equity and statute
To clarify these concepts, it may be helpful to illustrate them with reference to specific aspects of criminal and civil law.

- *The criminal offences of murder, conspiracy and incitement to commit a crime are all contrary to* common law. *No Acts have been passed which state that they are offences, although there is legislation which relates to them, such as the penalty to be applied when a person is convicted of murder.*

- *In contrast, the criminal offences of theft, forgery and assault are all contrary to* statute, *in that Parliament has passed legislation which specifically defines them as offences. As society has become more complex, most criminal offences are now subject to statute, although many important ones were originally common law offences.*

- *Many civil causes of action, including breach of contract, trespass, negligence and debt, arise at* common law. *However, the rules which determine what constitutes negligence have been established in past court judgments, starting with the case of* Donoghue v. Stevenson, *which you researched in Chapter 1.*

- *Civil disputes about wills involve* equity.

- *An example of a civil cause of action arising from* statute *is divorce. As we saw in Chapter 1, when the foundations of our legal system were laid, marriage was for life, and so after it was decided that there should be a means by which a marriage could be dissolved, Parliament had to pass legislation which defined the grounds on which it could be permitted.*

Public and private law

In suggesting that public law and private law can be contrasted, many lawyers would not understand what you were talking about. For most lawyers, public law describes the work done in the Administrative Court of the High Court – judicial review. So, again you can see that confusion can result from using the same expression in different senses. The expression *public law*, in contrast to *private law*, is relevant to family law proceedings under the Children Act 1989, in that public law applications are those in which a local authority is taking action in respect of a child, and private law applications involve disputes between private individuals, usually the parents.

Powers and duties

This distinction is clear and important. Both powers and duties arise under statutes. Other sources of law do not impose powers and duties, in the sense that the two concepts are contrasted. At common law, however, there is an important duty to take reasonable care not to cause damage, and failure to perform this duty is negligence. If a statute imposes a duty upon a person or organisation, it is an absolute requirement to do it. On the other hand, if a statute gives a power to a person or organisation, they may do it, but they do not have to. In many cases involving local authorities, courts have said that they cannot just ignore powers, but must actively consider whether to exercise them or not.

Whether a provision in a statute amounts to a power or a duty should be clear. Although lawyers are trained to interpret Acts of Parliament, all Acts are supposed to be understood by people who might need to read them, if necessary with the help of the increasingly detailed explanatory notes which accompany them. If you read in an Act that *it shall be the duty of X* to do something, or the word *must* is used, the provision in question is likely to be a duty. On the other hand, if the Act uses the word *may*, it is almost certainly a power. It can be tricky, however, if the word *shall* is used, without it being stated that it *shall be a duty*. Depending upon the context, the problem with *shall* is whether the word is mandatory, which means that it must be done, or directory, which means that it ought to be done, but it may not matter too much if it isn't.

ACTIVITY *4.1*

Obtain a copy of any legislation or policy applicable to your work or placement setting.

- *Do you think that the provisions contained in it are powers or duties?*

- *If it is unclear, what possible consequences might result?*

In the course of this activity, you may find that even if the distinction between powers and duties is fairly clear, other aspects of the documents are less easy to interpret. For example, what will happen if a duty is not carried out? Who decides, and on what basis, whether powers are to be exercised? This may go some way towards explaining why lawyers seem to be so focused on the meaning of words.

Negligence

Negligence in law just means carelessness. For example, if you drive your car into another car because you are not concentrating, you have damaged the other car as a result of your negligence – your carelessness. A duty to be careful is more likely to exist if the possible consequence of carelessness is that a person may be harmed or property damaged, rather than that someone loses money. This does not mean that you cannot ever be found legally liable for carelessness if you have not caused damage to a person or property, but it is unlikely. Essentially, to be found to have been careless when someone has lost only money as a consequence, you must have given advice to that person and failed to take care in the advice which you gave. It is not careless to be wrong, it is only wrong to be careless. As long as any advice which you give is advice which any reasonably competent social worker would give, there should be no problem.

Barristers used to be immune from allegations of negligence, at least in relation to what they did in court, but they are now liable in the same way as any other professional, as are solicitors and solicitor advocates. Barristers in private practice and solicitors must all be insured against professional negligence claims.

Expressions you may hear in court

What people are called

Advocate Either a barrister or a solicitor who presents a case in court. This is different from the advocate who may assist clients in arguing for their entitlement in a tribunal or their needs in a care home. The expression was not much used until solicitors began to present cases in court.

Barrister We explained the role and types of barrister in Chapter 2.

Clerk Other than in magistrates' courts, court clerks are not legally qualified, even though in robed hearings in the High Court they wear a wig and gown. In the High Court, clerks are called *associates* and their duties include recording the times of court sittings, swearing in witnesses and preparing the formal order at the conclusion of the hearing. County Courts do not have clerks in the formal sense, and if anyone is in court along with the judge and usher, it is likely to be a court administrator.

Legal executive Someone who works for a solicitors' practice or other legal department, but who is not a qualified solicitor. However, there is an Institute of Legal Executives whose members are qualified, but at a lower level of expertise than solicitors. Only members of the Institute should be referred to as legal executives, but in practice terminology is lax.

My friend How a barrister who is appearing in a case against a solicitor refers to the solicitor in court. In court lawyers traditionally do not refer to each other by name, either formally or informally.

My learned friend How a barrister refers to another barrister in court.

Para-legal A rather grand term for people who do photocopying, prepare documents and carry heavy boxes. They first appeared in the 1980s and were often law students on a gap year. It was said that their terms of payment was all the beer they could drink, which devalues the important service they provide to lawyers in preparing for court hearings.

Solicitor We explained the role of a solicitor in relation to court proceedings in Chapter 2.

Usher The person who makes sure everyone is in the right place at the right time, provides drinking water and, in some courts, swears in witnesses.

Hearings

In chambers A hearing from which the public and press are excluded. The term is now usually only used in family cases. Any other hearings to which the press and public are not admitted are usually described as *in private*.

Unrobed A hearing which is open to all, but in which the judge and lawyers do not wear robes. This is usually a preliminary hearing of some sort.

Robed A hearing which is open to all, in which the judge and the lawyers wear robes. All trials are like this, other than in family cases, although there are changes proposed in relation to civil trials (see Chapter 8).

Application A hearing, other than the trial, in which a party is seeking a court order, which could arise from anything connected with the preparation for trial. The hearing is unrobed.

Case management conference A hearing in a civil or family case at which arrangements for the trial are determined.

Directions hearing Technically an application, where the focus is on deciding what steps are needed to prepare the case for trial, such as exchanging documents and filing witness statements. The hearing is unrobed.

Plea and case management hearing, or PCMH A Crown Court hearing at which the accused person has to say whether they admit any of the charges against them and at which arrangements for the trial are made.

Pre-trial review A hearing shortly before trial at which a judge considers the state of preparation of the case and its readiness for trial.

Trial The hearing of either a criminal or a civil case, at which the evidence is heard and the legal argument about the issues takes place.

Other legal terms

Accused A person facing a criminal charge or charges. The term *defendant* is also used.

Acknowledgment of service The formal step by which a party who is being sued in a civil action records that they have received the relevant documents, and states whether they intend to admit or dispute the action.

Acquit Find an accused person in a criminal case not guilty.

Adjournment A temporary suspension of the hearing. This can be a break for lunch or at the end of the day, after which the hearing will continue when the court next sits, or a break for days or weeks to enable some action to be taken.

Administration Order A County Court order which directs a person to pay a specified amount into court in respect of outstanding debts.

Affidavit A written statement of evidence, confirmed on oath or by affirmation to be true and sworn before someone who has authority to administer it.

Affirmation Declaration by a witness with no religious beliefs, or religious beliefs that prevent them from taking the oath, that the evidence that they will give is true.

Alternative Dispute Resolution, or ADR A process of trying to resolve a dispute by compromise. This is a generic term which covers the variety of ways in which it can be done. See Chapter 2.

Annul Declare no longer valid.

Appellant Person who appeals.

Applicant Person who makes an application.

Bail Release of a person from custody until their next court appearance, usually subject to conditions.

Bailiff County Court officer, empowered to serve documents and execute warrants.

Brief Written instructions to a barrister, usually prepared by a solicitor.

Claim Proceedings issued in the County or High Court.

Claim form The formal step by which a civil action is started. Previously known in the High Court as a writ.

Claimant Person issuing a claim. Previously known as plaintiff.

Contempt of court Wilful disregard of the judicial process, which can be punished.

Convict Find an accused person in a criminal trial guilty. A person is still convicted if they admit a charge.

Cross-examination The questioning of a witness by an advocate for a party other than the one on whose behalf the witness has been called to give evidence. See Chapter 10.

Corroboration Evidence which confirms or supports that of a witness.

Court of Protection Due to be established under the Mental Capacity Act 2005 to determine disputes relating to capacity. It will operate from a central registry, but can sit anywhere in the country.

Damages Money claimed or awarded as compensation for physical or material loss.

Defendant An accused person in a criminal trial or, in a civil case, the person against whom a claim form has been issued.

Disclosure The process of listing relevant documents in a civil case, with a view to showing other parties what documents you have. See Chapter 5.

Divisional Court In addition to having their own original jurisdiction, all three divisions of the High Court can hear some appeals from lower courts and tribunals. Some types of appeal are heard by a Divisional Court of, usually, two judges.

Evidence in chief Evidence which the party calling a witness wants the witness to give and which they are prepared to give. In civil and family cases it is given in writing, called a witness statement. In criminal cases it is given by answering questions put by the advocate for the party calling the witness.

Hearsay Evidence which was not perceived by the witness's own senses. Usually it is evidence which a witness cannot confirm is true, because it was told to them by someone else. See Chapter 5.

Injunction A court order which prevents someone from doing something or, exceptionally, requires someone to do something. Breach of an injunction is contempt of court.

Inspection The process of allowing a party to whom you have given disclosure to read the listed documents, which is usually done by providing photocopies. See Chapter 5.

Interim Pending a full order or decision.

Litigant in person Someone who conducts their case in court without being legally represented.

Mediation Seeking to settle a dispute by using a mediator to try to bring the parties together.

Mitigation Reasons given on behalf of someone found guilty to excuse or explain the offence in an attempt to minimise the sentence imposed, or steps taken to reduce a loss which has been suffered.

Oath A verbal promise by a person with religious beliefs to tell the truth.

Official Receiver A civil servant whose function is to act as liquidator when a company is being wound up, or as trustee when someone is made bankrupt.

Official Solicitor The lawyer who represents people in legal proceedings who are not able to manage their own affairs.

Ouster An order which requires a person to leave a property.

Part 20, Part 20 claimant, Part 20 defendant Sometimes a person who is made a party in court proceedings wishes to make a claim against someone else in relation to the same matter. For example, if you are sued for damaging someone's car, you would want to claim on your own insurance in case you are found liable to pay for the damage. This procedure is permitted by Part 20 of the Civil Procedure Rules. The person making the claim against the new party is the Part 20 claimant and the person against whom it is made is the Part 20 defendant. The same procedure applies if a defendant in a civil claim wants to make a cross-claim against the claimant.

Party Participant in a court action.

Ratio or ratio decidendi Ratio is short for *ratio decidendi,* meaning *the reasoning needing to be decided.* The ratio is the legal reasoning established in a precedent. This Latin expression has not been replaced by another form of words.

Re-examination The re-questioning by a party who has called a witness to give evidence, after the conclusion of the cross-examination.

Respondent The party against whom an application or an appeal is made.

Sine die A Latin expression meaning *without a day,* used when an adjournment is agreed but no date for the resumed hearing is fixed.

Statement of truth A declaration at the end of a written statement of evidence that the contents are true.

Summing up A review of the evidence in a criminal trial and directions on the law by the judge before the jury considers its verdict.

Surety An undertaking to be liable for another person's default or non-attendance at court.

Suspended sentence A sentence which does not take effect unless a subsequent offence is committed within a specified period.

Ultra vires Acting in excess of authority, doing something which there is no power to do.

Witness statement See evidence in chief.

CHAPTER SUMMARY

In this chapter we have explained the legal concepts and expressions which you are most likely to meet. Although the legal profession is slowly adapting its language, there will still be times when you are unsure about the meaning of what you read or hear, and some words in common use may be understood differently in a legal context. If this happens, we strongly encourage you to ask for an explanation, since no one can take a full part in any process if they do not understand what is going on, and in some circumstances you may be the only person who can help interpret a legal procedure to someone who is directly involved in it. Needing to ask for clarification does not reflect on your competence and should offer a timely reminder to the lawyers of the need to think more carefully about the language they use.

FURTHER READING

There are numerous introductory books on law (A-level texts are probably best), all of which will enable you to read more about legal concepts and expressions.

WEBSITE

www.hmcourts-service.gov.uk/infoabout/glossary/legal
Contains a glossary of legal terms.

Chapter 5
Court rules

Introduction

Here we introduce various legal rules which affect the conduct of court proceedings. They are important because they will affect how the party on whose behalf you are involved must conduct itself, and because they also affect other parties. Rules can be daunting if you do not understand them. However, they also offer structure, consistency and a certain degree of predictability.

Disclosure and inspection of documents

Ordinary civil cases

In ordinary civil litigation, other than in family cases, each party must usually show the other parties any documents which are relevant to the dispute, because documents which existed at the time that events occurred usually shed a great deal of light on what actually happened. This has been the case for many years and is not just a recent development arising from open government or freedom of information. Because it has been the practice for so long, there has been plenty of argument as to what exactly needs to be revealed. You can safely leave these finer points to the lawyers, but it is useful to know what is involved in the process and the important exceptions. A document means anything in which information is recorded, and includes not only paper but electronic records, tape recordings, photographs and films. Today e-mails are regularly included, as are text messages and voicemails.

A party shows other parties its documents in two stages:

- a list of them is provided, known as *disclosure*;

- the other parties are allowed to see the documents which have been disclosed, which is called *inspection*.

Which documents have to be disclosed?

In ordinary civil litigation, all the documents on which the party making disclosure relies in support of its own case and any which adversely affect its case, or the case of another party, must be disclosed. Each party is likely to have the documents on which it is relying, or at least copies of them, but it may no longer have other types of documents which it ought to disclose. You do not avoid the need to disclose documents just because you no longer have them. However, you are only required to make a reasonable search for documents on which you yourself do not intend to rely. If several copies of a document exist, like a memorandum copied to a number of people, it is not necessary to disclose each copy, but any copy which contains modification, obliteration or other marking is treated as a separate document.

There are exceptions to the obligation to show documents to the other parties, in which case, although they must still be listed in the disclosure statement, they do not have to be made available for inspection. Obviously you do not need to show a document which you no longer have. Also, documents do not need to be disclosed if public interest immunity, legal professional privilege, litigation privilege or the without prejudice rules apply (see below). Solicitors used to send their trainees to look at other parties' documents, which sometimes revealed interesting material on the reverse. Now it is usual to provide photocopies or electronic copies, but anything on the reverse of the original must be included. The duty of disclosure continues throughout the proceedings, which means that any relevant document which was missed the first time and later turns up must be disclosed.

What use can be made of documents disclosed in the course of litigation?

Fortunately, rights to make use of them are restricted. A party to whom documents have been disclosed can only use them for the purposes of the proceedings in which the disclosure took place, unless the document has been read to or by the court, or referred to at a public hearing, or the court gives permission for another use of the document, or the party who disclosed it and the party to whom it belongs agree to it being used for another purpose. Even if a document has been read to or by the court, or referred to at a public hearing, the court may still restrict or prohibit its use.

Making a false disclosure statement is a contempt of court.

Family cases

In family cases there is no obligation to give general disclosure of the type described in other civil cases. Instead, if disclosure is necessary for the fair disposal of the proceedings, a party can be ordered to give disclosure of specific documents. However, in all cases involving children, the parties and their lawyers have a duty to make frank disclosure.

Criminal cases

The basic rule in criminal cases is that the prosecution must disclose to the defence all relevant documents. In the Crown Court, and in some types of cases heard by magistrates, the defence has to disclose the nature of the defence, but not the evidence which will be relied on to support it. There are separate procedures for the seizure of documents by the police to use as evidence with which we need not be concerned. However, the first two exceptions to the general rule of disclosure in ordinary civil cases covered below also apply to protect documents from seizure by the police, so that documents which are covered by public interest immunity or legal professional privilege should not be seized.

Public interest immunity

One of the grounds on which a party can withhold a document, which would otherwise need to be disclosed, is if public interest immunity applies. This principle applies in cases where breach of confidentiality in a document will cause harm to the public interest which is greater than the harm to the public interest caused by non-disclosure, illustrated by the following case.

CASE EXAMPLE

D v. *National Society for the Prevention of Cruelty to Children* [1978] AC 171

The NSPCC received a report that a child was being ill-treated. Following investigation, it was decided that the allegation was unfounded and the child's mother wanted to know who had made it, so that she could sue the person concerned. The NSPCC refused to say and the House of Lords decided that NSPCC records were covered by public interest immunity, because the work of the NSPCC depended on people being confident that they could report cases without their identity subsequently being revealed.

Public interest immunity can also apply to social work case records and applies in criminal cases as well as in civil and family cases, so documents which fall within this immunity do not need to be produced in criminal proceedings either. However, the fact that a document is protected by public interest immunity does not mean that it needs to be kept confidential. Any document which is referred to by a witness must be disclosed and consequently, in most cases in which you are involved, your case records are likely to be disclosed as part of the evidence. In childcare cases the presumption is against a local authority relying upon public interest immunity. Children's guardians always have a right to see local authority records.

Legal professional privilege

We considered in Chapter 3 the professional rules which require barristers and solicitors to keep their clients' information confidential. Next we consider the entitlement of people to keep confidential their exchanges with their own lawyers.

It is a fundamental legal principle that people should be able to consult lawyers freely and frankly, confident that what they have told them will not be passed on to anyone else without their consent. A Victorian Master of the Rolls, Sir George Jessel, in *Anderson* v. *Bank of British Columbia* [1876] 2 ChD 644, explained why this principle is needed:

> *The object and meaning of the rule is this: that as, by reason of the complexity and difficulty of our law, litigation can only be properly conducted by professional men, it is absolutely necessary that a man, in order to prosecute his rights or to defend himself from an improper claim, should have recourse to the*

assistance of professional lawyers, and it being so absolutely necessary, it is equally necessary, to use a vulgar phrase, that he should be able to make a clean breast of it to the gentleman whom he consults with a view to the prosecution of his claim, or the substantiating his defence against the claim of others; that he should be able to place unrestricted and unbounded confidence in the professional agent, and that the communications he so makes to him should be kept secret, unless with his consent ... that he should be enabled properly to conclude his litigation.

The courts have recognised that the administration of justice is impossible without legal professional privilege and so no one else is ever entitled to know what legal advice has been sought or given about anything. It applies to all legal advice, not just in the context of litigation, so advice received about possible courses of action before there is any question of litigation is also privileged. Obviously, in an organisation like a local authority, legal advice may have to be shared among several people. The privilege is not lost by doing that, even if someone who is not a lawyer summarises to another person what the lawyer has said. However, subject to the possibility that such a document may be covered by public interest immunity, ordinary communications between staff of a social work agency, or between one department and another, are not privileged unless they relate to the giving or receiving of legal advice.

Litigation privilege

While legal advice is always privileged, an additional type of privilege applies only in relation to preparing a case for a hearing, called litigation privilege. This applies to documents which have been produced principally in order to give or receive advice, or to collect evidence in connection with actual or anticipated litigation. The privilege therefore covers witness statements and experts' reports in ordinary civil litigation, until the moment it is decided to provide copies of the documents to the other parties. Consequently, in ordinary civil litigation, drafts of witness statements and experts' reports are covered by litigation privilege. It also covers requests for evidence, for example by letter, and responses to such requests. However, in children's cases, there is no litigation privilege in relation to experts' reports. This is both because of the non-adversarial nature of such proceedings and also because the consent of the court is required to disclose documents to the expert, or to have the child examined.

CASE EXAMPLE

In Re L (a minor) (police investigation) [1997] AC 16, two parents, who were addicted to heroin, obtained permission to show court papers to a chemical pathologist, hoping to demonstrate that their two-year-old child could have ingested methadone accidentally. The pathologist, however, did not support this contention, and his report had to be disclosed to the court concerned with the child's welfare, against the wishes of the parents.

In criminal cases the defendant can always rely on litigation privilege. However, the prosecution has to disclose any material assembled in anticipation of the trial which it decides not to use. This is called *unused material*.

Without prejudice communications

In civil and family cases the law aims to promote settlement of disputes and avoid expensive and potentially damaging trials. Consequently, documents produced with a view to negotiating a settlement are privileged from disclosure if settlement is not achieved. Of course, the parties to the negotiations will each have copies of all the documents, so the principle is really about none of them being able to refer in court to what has been said during the negotiations. Subject to limited exceptions, the negotiations cannot even be referred to if there is in fact a settlement. For many years lawyers have written at the top of letters about negotiations *without prejudice*, but this formula does not have to be used. If a document is a part of negotiations aimed at achieving a settlement, it is privileged whether the words *without prejudice* are used or not. On the other hand, using those words does not make the document privileged if it is not a part of a negotiation aimed at a settlement. Sometimes people include the words *without prejudice* when they hope that what is written will not be held against them. This is not the proper purpose of the privilege, and such documents are not protected from being put in evidence in court.

ACTIVITY **5.1**

You are a social worker on a local authority leaving and after-care team, and you are supporting Nathan, 18, who is living in a privately rented furnished bedsit. One weekend he has a party at which his friend gets very drunk and breaks a plate glass door. Nathan refuses to pay for the damage as it was not his fault. However, the landlord decides to sue him for the costs of repair and Nathan is worried that he will lose his accommodation. He wants to make an offer to the landlord, in the hope of settling the matter before it gets to court. However, he is worried that if he does this, he will be admitting that he is responsible and will then be liable for the whole amount, plus any court costs. In the light of what we have explained about without prejudice communications, what do you think Nathan should do?

Of course, the landlord may not be willing to negotiate, but legal action is never risk-free for any party, and this exercise demonstrates that knowing the rules can potentially be of assistance to service users in particular circumstances.

Hearsay

Hearsay is evidence of what someone has told you, rather than evidence of what you saw, heard, smelled, touched or tasted yourself. If it is relevant to know what someone said to you, as opposed to whether what they said was accurate, evidence of this is not hearsay. If a child told you that they were being bullied at school, you could offer that as evidence of what they told you, but not as evidence of the fact that they were being bullied. The rules of hearsay are important in criminal cases, but less so in civil cases, and rules made under the Children Act 1989 gave courts the power to allow hearsay evidence in cases involving the welfare of children. If there is an issue of whether evidence is hearsay or not, the legal rules governing what can be said can be quite complicated. However, you do not need to worry about them, even if you are giving evidence in a criminal case. If the lawyers think that your answers are inadmissible as evidence, it is for them or the judge to deal with it.

ACTIVITY **5.2**

Consider the policy and practice in your placement agency or workplace which relates to the making and sharing of records:

- *How far does it take account of the sort of court rules we have outlined?*

- *In compiling your records, what actions would be sensible preparation against the possibility that they might become subject to these rules?*

Most agencies have policies which support the sharing of records with service users, and this principle is supported by legislation. However, in practice they are widely ignored. Anticipating the possibility that your records might need to be disclosed in the course of court proceedings is an effective way of achieving the standards required. Reading other people's recordings with a critical eye and assessing how far they might stand up to challenge will also support the development of your recording skills.

Exposure of witnesses to liability as a result of giving evidence

You may be concerned as to what extent you may be exposed as a result of giving evidence in court. In particular, you may wonder whether, if the case for the party on whose behalf you are appearing is unsuccessful, you could be sued for libel or slander. (Libel is defamatory material in a document, while slander is defamation of someone by spoken word.) Occasionally, people have tried to retaliate against witnesses who have spoken against them, and so you will be relieved to know that the rules are clear. Essentially you have nothing to fear, unless, of course, what you say is untrue.

In criminal proceedings, unless statements are made which are nothing to do with the prosecution, witnesses are totally immune from being sued. In civil proceedings, witnesses have absolute privilege against exposure to defamation, and witness statements cannot be used for any purpose other than the proceedings in which they are served, unless the witness consents, the court gives permission or the statement has been put in evidence at a public hearing. Consequently, if someone gets to hear of the content of a witness statement, which is not in the event put forward in evidence, they cannot rely on it, for example in support of a claim for defamation, without either the consent of the witness (who will not give it) or the court, which would be very unlikely to give permission solely in order to enable an aggrieved person to sue.

Evidence of children and vulnerable adults

As a social worker you may be involved in supporting someone who needs to be a witness in court, and consequently you need to know what special provisions can be made, and in what circumstances. In 1998 a Home Office working group on the treatment of vulnerable or intimidated witnesses in the criminal justice system produced its report, *Speaking Up for Justice,* which resulted in Part II of the Youth Justice and Criminal Evidence Act 1999. This introduces a number of special measures which may be made available to witnesses, in criminal proceedings only, who satisfy the following criteria set out in ss. 16 and 17 of the Act, that is who:

- are not the accused person in the case; and

- are under 17; or

- have a mental disorder or significant impairment of intelligence and social functioning which the court considers likely to affect the quality of their evidence; or

- have a physical disorder or disability which the court considers likely to affect the quality of their evidence; or

- are a person, the quality of whose evidence the court considers likely to be diminished by fear or distress in connection with giving evidence in the case. A complainant in a case involving a possible sexual offence automatically fulfils this condition, but does not have to take advantage of it.

There are various special measures which can be taken, for example:

- screens to prevent the witness seeing the accused, although they must not prevent the witness being seen by the judge, jury and lawyers acting in the proceedings;

- taking the evidence in private, but obviously in the presence of the judge and jury or magistrates, the accused and the lawyers;

- removal of wigs and robes worn by the judge and lawyers;

- giving of some, or all, of the evidence by means of a live or pre-recorded video link;

- use of an intermediary to convey questions and answers;

- use of a device to enable the witness to receive questions and communicate answers.

In deciding whether special measures should be provided, the court must take into account the views of the witness concerned and consider whether the proposed measures are likely to improve the quality of the evidence or, conversely, inhibit evidence being effectively given.

A further element of witness protection provided by the Act is that of preventing an unrepresented person accused of a sexual offence from personally cross-examining the potential victim. A lawyer representing someone in these circumstances may not cross-examine the complainant about previous sexual history without the court's permission, which can only be given on limited grounds.

In civil and family proceedings, no formal measures exist to assist vulnerable witnesses. Under the Civil Evidence Act 1995, a written statement from any witness can be put in evidence, and so normally children and vulnerable adults would not need to give oral evidence. If it was considered important that a vulnerable witness should be cross-examined on their written evidence, the court could take steps to facilitate this and minimise the stress on them. If cross-examination was not possible, it might be the subject of comment in the context of the value (*weight*) of the evidence.

RESEARCH SUMMARY

Children can achieve 80–90 per cent recall when questioned in a supportive manner and in a relaxed environment fairly soon after an event (Westcott, 2006). Other factors found to promote accuracy include:

- use of open questions in preference to closed questions;

- avoidance of leading questions;

- avoidance of jargon and other complex language;

- clarification of expectations;

- a friendly manner and positive non-verbal communication, including eye contact, on the part of the interviewer.

ACTIVITY 5.3

Ask colleagues or friends, of varying ages and backgrounds, what they know about court rules:

- *What is the source of the information?*

- *What connotations does it have for them?*

- *What do they think is the purpose of court rules?*

- *What do they think will happen if any of the rules are not followed?*

- *If they had to be a witness in court, what would concern them most in relation to court rules?*

- *Where do they think they could get help in understanding court rules?*

When you have done this, compile a list of the most common responses. This will then provide you with a framework with which to prepare and support people involved in court proceedings.

C H A P T E R   S U M M A R Y

In this chapter we have explained some of the legal rules which you are most likely to be concerned about, or meet, in the course of court proceedings. Although they may at first seem unfamiliar concepts, most of them are rooted in a foundation of fairness, transparency and openness, principles which also underpin social work. They can be a useful checklist when compiling your case records or communicating professionally in writing, and being familiar with them will help you support anyone involved in legal proceedings.

WEBSITES

www.cjsonline.gov.uk

The cross-departmental Office for Criminal Justice Reform offers support to criminal justice agencies and people involved in the criminal justice system. It manages a register of qualified intermediaries to support witnesses and victims, and its website contains preparatory materials such as virtual court tours.

www.nspcc.org.uk

The NSPCC publishes preparatory materials, such as videos and board games, to help prepare children for giving evidence.

www.victimsupport.org.uk

Victim Support's witness service operates in every Crown Court to give information and support to witnesses, victims, their family and friends. It is free and confidential, and normally contacts potential witnesses in advance of any court hearing.

Chapter 6
Preparing for court

Introduction

The focus of this chapter is how to prepare for court once proceedings are not a theoretical possibility but a likelihood. You will probably be surprised at how much is involved, but attention to detail at this stage will pay dividends when you reach the hearing itself.

Who has to be prepared?

Often the only thing that families involved in care proceedings feel they have in common with the social workers is that they are all nervous of court processes. If the social workers are too well-prepared, they won't even have that. (Parents' Aid representative)

Usually you are involved in a court case because one of your clients is. Therefore not only do you have to prepare yourself, but you may have to support your client or someone who is involved with your client, like a foster carer. People who are looking to you for support will be reassured if you are familiar with the process and understand what is likely to happen. Additionally your managers and legal advisers will be undertaking their own preparation, and you will need to communicate with them about it.

55

When and why do you have to be prepared?

Sometimes it is necessary to respond to an emergency and you have to react to a process which has been started by someone else. However, you are most likely to be involved in legal proceedings because your employer, usually a local authority, has decided to initiate them. If there is a choice, the obvious decision is not to start proceedings until you are ready, which is when legal advice has been taken and all the evidence necessary to support the case has been assembled.

In family cases involving children, there are timescales which courts expect the parties to adhere to. This is to comply with the requirements of s.1(2) of the Children Act 1989 that *the court shall have regard to the general principle that any delay in determining the question is likely to prejudice the welfare of the child*. However, the complexity of the decision-making processes involved, particularly if the final hearing is joined to a placement application by the local authority, makes it increasingly difficult to prepare properly and meet the deadlines while at the same time maintaining the rest of your caseload.

> *You haven't got time to sit down and physically go through everything any more.*
>
> (Social worker, quoted by Beckett et al., 2007)

Procedural difficulties, such as experts' reports which are delayed or not shared with other parties, can exacerbate the problem. Timely supervision will provide the opportunity to think through and reflect on the professional dilemmas and personal challenges which may arise, and your manager's support is essential in order to ensure that the planning and decision-making is undertaken thoroughly and everyone is kept fully informed.

> **CASE EXAMPLE**
>
> *In the course of care proceedings, the magistrate asked the social worker what she thought would be the impact on the child of being separated from the parents, and the social worker replied,* None. *Afterwards, the children's guardian and expert witness asked the social worker whether this was really what she believed, and she replied,* Well, I was put on the spot, and I couldn't think what to say.

With the support of good supervision and proper preparation, the social worker might have anticipated this kind of question and been able to give an informed response. As it was, she let herself down, did nothing for the reputation of her profession and, most importantly, overlooked the interests of the child. We suggest that, as soon as court proceedings appear likely, you draw up a personal timetable, which includes all the deadlines of which you are aware, and builds in the time required to prepare and update statements, attend meetings, seek supervision and undertake all the necessary investigation, reading and checking.

Legal advice

You may not be in a position to ask for legal advice directly yourself, but you should emphasise to those who are that advice should be sought once you feel that a case may be moving towards legal proceedings. Your employers are likely to have a legal section with lawyers experienced in dealing with the sorts of cases which your department is likely to produce, and they can also access outside lawyers for more specialist advice. If legal advice is sought at a relatively early stage, when it seems likely that the case will have to go to court, but before it is urgently necessary, it is possible to consider it in a calm atmosphere, and to assess, jointly with the lawyers, what sort of evidence you have, who can provide it and whether it will support a case being brought, which may involve liaison with other agencies. Similarly, if you are supporting someone facing a criminal charge or other court action, it is important to know where to go to get the right sort of advice (see Chapter 13).

Legal representation

In addition to taking legal advice before any proceedings are started, the parties involved will need to be represented at any hearing. You will not have to arrange this, but you will almost certainly have to collaborate closely with the legal representatives in preparing the case for court. What might this involve?

First, you are likely to have meetings with the legal representatives, or they will attend a planning meeting. If it is decided to instruct a barrister (counsel), there will almost certainly be a solicitor from the local authority's legal department, or from an outside firm, involved. The solicitor will need access to the case file and will want to meet with you. A statement from you will almost certainly be necessary. This will probably not be the statement which eventually is put before the court as your evidence, but it is the best way in which to tell the lawyers about the issues in the case. Although you can be guided as to what needs to be covered in your statement, you must write this yourself. You should take notice of any comments about additional matters which should be included, or any use of language which the solicitor suggests is unclear. Apart from that, be careful. Be very, very cautious about agreeing to leave out something which you think should be included and there is a considerable risk of you being criticised if you do. The solicitor is unlikely to be criticised, because it is your statement, not theirs (see Chapter 7).

If a barrister has been brought in (*instructed*) to present the case, you will probably be asked to attend a meeting with them, called a *conference* when it is with a junior barrister, or a *consultation* when it is with a QC. Usually conferences or consultations take place in the barrister's chambers which, if you work near London, are likely to be in London. Depending upon how complex the case is, you may have to attend a number of such meetings.

There are two principal purposes of a conference or a consultation:

- to enable the barrister to obtain information about the case from those with first-hand knowledge; and
- to give legal advice.

It is therefore likely that several people will attend, some of whom know about the facts of the case, and others who are responsible for decisions about how the case should be conducted, in the light of advice given. It is not the barrister's responsibility to make investigations into the facts of a case, or to collect evidence for use in court. Barristers therefore do not normally interview witnesses in order to discover what evidence they would give at a trial. The purpose of people with factual knowledge attending a meeting with a barrister is so that the barrister knows the facts on which advice is being sought.

Once legal representation has been arranged, the lawyers must be kept up to date with developments in the case, so that they can give further advice or reconsider advice already given. Again, you might not make contact directly with lawyers (and some employers restrict this in order to contain costs), but you should make sure that your manager knows if there have been developments which you think are important.

Relationships between lawyers and social workers

A potential area of tension is the precise nature of the relationship between you and the lawyers representing you, or more usually your employer as it is they who will pay the bill. In most lawyer/client relationships, the client gives instructions, considers the advice offered and decides how to proceed in the light of this advice. However, it can sometimes be unclear as to who exactly is the client (you, your line manager a service manager or your employer as a whole, who might also be the lawyer's employer), and although it depends on the personalities and experience of those involved, you may need to clarify your position and the decision-making process in your agency at the outset. Equally significant as a potential source of confusion is the rapid pace of organisational change within social care agencies. Many judges, magistrates and lawyers, and indeed anyone not directly involved in providing social work services, will not be as up to date as you are in relation to changes in management structure and, for example, will continue to regard social services as a generic organisation long after the service has been split into separate service areas.

> ## CASE EXAMPLE
>
> *In a case where the mother was looked-after by the local authority, the majority of the cross-examination on behalf of the mother, and also the children's guardian, was about the services, or lack of services, provided to the mother, even though this was not my team's responsibility. We also got questioned about the services being offered, or not offered, by other teams, such as the adult learning disability service. (Child protection team manager)*

Again, it is worth explaining to the lawyers in your case any recent changes in the organisation of your agency which have had an impact on the responsibilities held by different departments, budgetary decisions and how services are planned and delivered.

RESEARCH SUMMARY

Dickens (2005, 2006) has explored how local authority social workers, social services managers and lawyers work together in childcare cases. He found that generally inter-professional relationships worked well, but that tensions were never far from the surface. The strongest criticisms from social workers were directed at lawyers who were not supportive, or who appeared unwilling to listen to, and respect, the social worker's opinions. Less experienced social workers, and those who did not feel they were getting sufficient guidance from their own managers, were likely to look to the lawyers for high levels of practical and emotional support, and most also wanted the lawyers to be strong advocates in court. Lawyers, however, sometimes felt unhappy about being drawn into social work issues, and one described the dilemma they faced in balancing their responsibility to the court with the instructions received from their client: *It clearly got to the stage where I wasn't advising on legal issues at all … . I was trying to prop someone up who wasn't receiving support from their own manager.*

Brammer (2007, p102) suggests that barriers to effective relationships between social workers and lawyers would be reduced by joint training, multi-disciplinary interest groups, dissemination of information such as legal fact sheets and clarification of roles and responsibilities at the outset.

Relationships with children's guardians

RESEARCH SUMMARY

Beckett et al. (2007) found that it was often perceived by social workers that courts gave more weight to guardians' views, even if based on more limited evidence:

It's almost like the proceedings is the start of involvement. They don't see involvement as being you've tried for years to make a difference with this family. You can give them a load of history … and it just seems to be wiped away.

I've heard the judge say 'this is the expert on the child'. And you just sit there and your blood boils.

It's nine times out of ten guaranteed that guardians have more status within the court proceedings than a social worker who has far more contact with the child and the family.

However, Stanley (2004) found that overt disagreement between professionals was rare, and differences of opinion as between children's guardians and local authority social workers tended to be explored and negotiated positively.

Understanding each professional's different role in court proceedings, whatever their background or qualifications, is important. It is worth, for example, arranging a meeting with a children's guardian, family court adviser or local authority lawyer outside any actual court proceedings, to develop an understanding of their role and explore potential areas of misunderstanding or tension. Also important is an appreciation of the need for far-reaching decisions to be tested by as many means as possible, although this may conflict with the principle of avoiding delay. Ultimately, in many family proceedings, there is no *right* answer, or at least little possibility of a result that can be evaluated without the benefit of hindsight, and judges and magistrates have to accept the responsibility for the decisions they make. Beckett et al. (2007) argue that the quality of decision-making, and also, we would add, the challenge of working with others, would benefit from (our italics):

- a less adversarial approach *on the part of everyone involved, both inside and outside court*;

- better support for all participants (also highlighted by Dickens, 2006), *particularly service users*;

- information from the present being seen in the context of what has happened in the past, *particularly by experts, magistrates and judges*.

In addition, Dickens (2006, p30) concludes, and we agree, that the valuing of difference, rather than its avoidance or suppression, is at the heart of effective inter-professional court work:

> *Differences of opinion and ways of working can be productive, sometimes*
> *supporting workers and sometimes challenging them, but always pushing them*
> *to reflect on, and account for, their beliefs and practices.*

Most importantly, social workers can do much to enhance their professional credibility and relationships with others by continually working on identified areas of potential weakness, such as the writing of reports, and being receptive to other points of view.

Reports and files

The next chapter covers writing reports, and most of your case records will have been written long before you find yourself going to court. However, the case will inevitably be a continuing one, and there may be important developments before a court hearing. It is absolutely essential that your file is up to date when you go to court. It is no good telling the court that you have made recent visits which have not been recorded on file, or that there has been contact with a doctor or some other agency which you have not had time to note. Remind yourself of this with this advice: *if it isn't recorded, it didn't happen*.

Confidentiality

You already know that confidentiality is a core social work principle. However, your duty of confidentiality towards your client and others is overridden once it becomes necessary to seek legal advice. In other words, you should not normally hold back information from legal advisers on the grounds that you owe a duty of confidentiality towards a client or someone else. As we have seen, lawyers have a clear duty of confidentiality towards their clients, so you ought to feel confident that anything you say to them about a client's affairs, or any doubts or concerns you express, will not go further.

Witness preparation

In England and Wales this is a sensitive subject. In the United States it is common for witnesses to be coached on how they should give their evidence, which involves mock cross-examination, based on the actual facts and issues in the case, and suggestions as to how particular questions should be answered. The whole exercise is designed to manipulate the witness's evidence so as to make it as favourable as possible. In England and Wales this is absolutely forbidden. What is permitted is one of the objects of this book, to familiarise witnesses with the layout of a court, the likely sequence of events at a hearing and the different responsibilities of the various participants. The Bar Council (2005) has produced guidance on witness preparation:

> 4. ... *Such arrangements* [that is, the familiarisation process just described] *prevent witnesses from being disadvantaged by ignorance of the process or being taken by surprise at the way in which it works, and so assist witnesses to give of their best at the trial or hearing in question, without any risk that their evidence may become anything other than the witnesses' own uncontaminated evidence ...*

> 5. ... *it is also appropriate, as part of a witness familiarisation process, for barristers to advise witnesses as to the basic requirements for giving evidence, e.g. the need to listen to and answer the question put, to speak clearly and slowly in order to ensure that the Court hears what the witness is saying, and to avoid irrelevant comments ...*

This guidance applies to you in two ways.

- You should not expect to be coached in your evidence and, if coaching is offered, you should refuse to have anything to do with it.

- You should not discuss with potential witnesses what their evidence is going to be or how they should answer particular questions. This does not mean that you cannot discuss the case or the issues in it; this would make your job impossible in any case which was likely to go to court. The important thing is to avoid making any suggestions about what the evidence should be, or how it should be given.

Support for the client

> *It is very harrowing for people to hear their most personal failures discussed publicly. Most clients are very fragile during court hearings, and it is very difficult to hold them together.* (Parents' Aid representative)

If you as a professional are anxious about involvement in legal proceedings and attending court, you can imagine how much more daunting it is likely to be for your client/s. For many of them, a great deal is at stake, which may affect their attitudes and behaviour. The whole process is likely to be bewildering, confusing and frightening, and there may be little you can do to reassure them. Certainly, if there is a disputed issue at stake, the traditional role of the social worker as supporter or advocate is unlikely to be possible, and despite your best efforts, communication may become very difficult.

> *Children and families may be supported through their involvement in safeguarding processes by advice and advocacy services, and they should always be informed of the services that exist locally and nationally.*

(DfES, 2006, p190)

Most people involved in legal proceedings are legally represented, but many lawyers are not primarily motivated by a wish to provide emotional support to their clients, and they vary in how competent, or interested, they are in this area. Although you may be preoccupied with your own anxieties, a person or organisation skilled in offering help and advice to people who are involved in particular types of legal proceedings can have a significant impact on their experience.

RESEARCH SUMMARY

An evaluation of the operation of the Children Act carried out by the Department of Health (Freeman and Hunt, 1998) found that most parents were ill-prepared for court proceedings and many found the experience intimidating and confusing. It was felt that there was potential for improving their experiences, despite their generally negative views.

A research report into the operation of Rule 9.5 of the Family Proceedings Rules 1991 describes children's experiences of family court proceedings. Researchers found that most children were confused by the court process, and believed that courts should enable children to express their wishes and feelings directly if they wanted to. Many parents were confused about the respective roles of the professionals involved (Douglas et al., 2006).

Practical arrangements

Part of preparing for court involves making practical arrangements to enable you to be at court throughout the hearing, without being distracted by other concerns. The first essential is to establish when any hearing is going to take place and how long it is likely to last. In a family case you are likely to be required for the whole of the length of the hearing and so you should ensure that you do not have conflicting professional or personal obligations at the relevant time. Most court hearings do not begin before 10.30 a.m. or continue after 4.30 p.m. However, magistrates and district judges sometimes operate outside these hours if it is necessary in order to finish a case. You need to take this into account, for example, in making any necessary domestic arrangements. Also, you need to allow sufficient time to travel to court and, if necessary, to park for the whole day.

The next example demonstrates the importance of taking account of the possibility of unexpected events and ensuring that adequate support is on hand when making practical arrangements.

CASE EXAMPLE

In care proceedings being heard in a magistrates' court, the local authority was represented by a private solicitor and a legal executive from the authority's legal department. The magistrates sat beyond the expected finish time in order to complete the case, which finally ended around 7 p.m. The decision not to make a care order was completely unexpected, which left the social worker without any support or effective legal advice about what to do next. While attempts were made to contact managers and a lawyer in the legal department, all the social worker could do was telephone the foster carer to warn them that the parents were coming to collect the child.

Finding the court building

The address of every court in the country, along with a photograph of the outside of the building, can be found on the website of HM Courts Service, which also gives telephone numbers and opening hours. In many cases, particularly in relation to County Courts, finding the building is only half the battle. Crown Courts and magistrates' courts usually have a building to themselves, or at least share only with other courts. Some County Courts share a building with other courts, but others occupy space in an office block alongside other businesses or organisations. Always allow plenty of time when going to court; not only are there the normal travelling hazards, but you need to take into account two additional features: security and finding the right court once you get to the building. Arriving late and flustered is not a good idea.

Security

For many years court buildings have been regarded as potential targets for terrorists. A car bomb exploded outside the Old Bailey in 1973 causing injuries to barristers, and since then airport-style security has been in place in all Crown Courts and in the Royal Courts of Justice. In most magistrates' and County Courts there is also security of some sort, and you may have your bags searched, have to pass through a metal detector, or even be subjected to a body search. You will speed up the procedure if you ensure that anything likely to set off the metal detector, such as a mobile phone, keys or loose change, is in your bag and not in your pocket. Court staff and judges all have security clearance and use different entrances from the general public. Barristers and solicitors, however, are subject to the same security procedures as anyone else. In some buildings there is an indication of the State of Alert posted on a board by the entrance. The normal State of Alert is Black, which simply indicates that there is a possibility of terrorist activity. Black Special indicates an increased risk, and may mean that security procedures are more rigorous. Higher States of Alert may result in courts being closed.

Finding the right court

The challenge of this task should not be underestimated. It is unlikely that there is a court left in the country which has only one courtroom. If your hearing is before a district judge in a County Court, or a Master or a Registrar in the High Court, the hearing will be in the judge's private room, and the notice of the hearing may say which that is. For some hearings taking place robed in open court, it is possible to find out on the afternoon of the day before the hearing where it will take place. Although you may know which judge is due to hear the case, few judges always sit in the same courtroom. In the High Court a cause list is published each afternoon in respect of the following day's sittings, which can be accessed on the HM Courts Service website. It is also possible to obtain free of charge on the internet details of some Crown Court hearings, and a comprehensive list of all court hearings other than in magistrates' courts is available to your legal advisers via various subscription websites. The designated court may change at any time before the hearing, so you need to check again when you arrive.

After passing through security, you may find that there is a notice board listing the day's cases. There are also usually signs in the larger courts indicating where each courtroom is to be found. However, if there is no list, the only thing to do is to ask. In magistrates' courts, and for hearings before district judges in County Courts, an usher will probably be in the waiting area, making a note of who has arrived for which case. For robed hearings in open court no one is likely to be noting down who has arrived, but the security personnel will probably be able to tell you where to go. If the hearing is in a private room, you will not be expected to go in until the time for your hearing. Some hearings may theoretically be open to the public, but the small size of the room usually means that it is not expected that anyone other than those involved will actually attend. If the hearing is in a courtroom, you could go and sit at the back if the court is open. Some courtrooms are open all the time the building is open, but others are only unlocked just before the start of each hearing.

The most difficult buildings to find your way around are those with the greatest number of different courts. A building which only contains magistrates' courts will typically have up to four courtrooms. A purpose-built Crown Court, in which no other courts sit, may have up to six courtrooms. A County Court in an office block will probably have two courtrooms, but also three or four rooms in which district judges hold hearings. These private rooms are likely to have a separate waiting area, so you need to find the right place to wait. There is also a type of building called a Combined Court Centre which contains both Crown and County Courts, and may also include magistrates' courts in a separate part of the building. The district judges' private rooms will also be in a separate part of the building. However, the courtrooms will be used for whatever cases are being heard on the day. In one court the Crown Court could be trying a murder case, and in the next-door court there could be a County Court hearing.

The Royal Courts of Justice (RCJ) are housed in four principal buildings on the main site: the Main block, the West Green Building, the Thomas More Building and the Queen's Building. The Main block is in two principal sections, the centre block and west block (which are really one), and the east block. Navigating around the RCJ is not for the faint-hearted: quite separate from the ways round which are available to the public and to lawyers is a network of corridors which can be used only by judges and staff. Over thirty years after learning the public ways round the RCJ, one of the authors had to find the way round the judges' corridors, with no one to ask and no signposts. The main public entrance to the RCJ is from the Strand, through the doors often photographed on television. The other public entrance is at the back, from Carey Street at first-floor level because the site slopes from back to front. The Strand entrance leads into the very grand main hall. The original courts, Courts 1–19, are at first-floor level in a ring around the main hall and are mostly used for trials in Queen's Bench or Chancery actions or for hearings of the Administrative Court. Courts 20–25 are in the basement of the west block, to the left of the main hall and courts 31–38A are in the West Green Building, reached from the rear of the main hall, by turning left under a covered walkway. Some family cases are heard in the West Green Building, but most take place in the Queen's Building, which houses Courts 39–50, 81 and 82. The entrance to the Queen's Building is to the right of the entrance to the West Green Building. In the Thomas More Building are Courts 51–62, 78 and 79, mostly used for trials of Chancery actions. In the east block are Courts 63–76, used either for Court of Appeal hearings or for trials of Queen's Bench actions. Queen's Bench Masters are found in the east block and Chancery Masters are in the Thomas More Building. Family Division Registrars are in the Principal Registry of the Family Division, in First Avenue House, Holborn, which also contains Court 80. St Dunstan's House, 200 yards from the RCJ, houses the Technology and Construction Court and some courts used by the Commercial Court.

What to wear at court

The guiding rule is that what you wear should not draw more attention to your clothing than to your evidence. You do not have to wear a suit, but you should dress in a way which is consistent with your professional status. For women, there is no need to wear a skirt or dress, rather than trousers or a dark colour, if you would be happier in something brighter. Most courts, however, expect men to wear a shirt and tie, rather than a sweater or T-shirt. Within reason, the shirt and tie can be any colour or pattern.

What not to wear

- jeans – ever;

- anything tight, short or revealing;

- anything in which you will not be comfortable sitting for a whole day;

- anything which might reinforce the stereotype of a social worker, like a flowing print skirt and long dangling earrings, or open-toed sandals.

Another point to bear in mind is that if you are attending court with your client, whether or not there is an issue of conflict between you, it is likely to reinforce your client's anxiety and apprehension, and increase their perception of the power differential between you, if your court clothes are very different from what you usually wear for work.

C H A P T E R   S U M M A R Y

This chapter has shown that there are a number of aspects of preparing for court, all of which require time and attention to detail. It is unlikely that busy practitioners will have all the time that they need to prepare as thoroughly as they would wish. However, keeping calm in the court environment is important, and it is more likely that you will manage this if you have anticipated the extent of preparation and planning required.

FURTHER READING

Cooper, P. (2006) *Reporting to the Court under the Children Act*, 2nd edn. London: Stationery Office. This text includes checklists which have been developed against practice directions and procedural rules and will help you adhere to a realistic timetable.

WEBSITES

www.hmcourts-service.gov.uk/courthearings.htm

www.courtnews2.co.uk/courtlists/current
Contain court listings for the following day.

www.parents-aid.org.uk
An organisation which provides support to families facing child protection investigation and court proceedings.

Chapter 7
Excellence in report writing

ACHIEVING A SOCIAL WORK DEGREE

This chapter addresses the communication skills defined within QAA subject benchmarks for social work, and will help you meet the following national occupational standards for social work:

Key role 1: Prepare for, and work with, individuals, families, carers, groups and communities to assess their needs and circumstances.

- Review case notes and other relevant literature.
- Assess needs, risks and options taking into account legal and other requirements.

Key role 5: Manage and be accountable, with supervision and support, for your own social work practice within your organisation.

- Carry out duties using accountable professional judgment and knowledge-based social work practice.
- Maintain accurate, complete, accessible and up-to-date records and reports.
- Provide evidence for judgments and decisions.

Introduction

This chapter is concerned with reports which may be also presented as witness statements.

Why strive for high standards in reporting to the court?

- to promote the best interests of the child;

- to provide accurate, accessible and relevant information;

- to provide a sound foundation for the action being requested from the court;

- because well-structured and clearly presented material is the best preparation for giving oral evidence;

- because all written material submitted to the court is automatically disclosed to all the parties before a hearing.

In the past, social work reports have been criticised for being unfocused, failing to distinguish between fact and opinion, reproducing large sections of case records with little structure or editing and, worst of all, failing to address the best interests of the child (Cooper, 2006, pp1–2).

RESEARCH SUMMARY

A review of judicial decision-making and the management of care proceedings in Northern Ireland found that:

> *Social work case files often contained a large amount of information about families that lacked a coherent family overview or history. Chronologies were thought by the authors to be necessary, but were often only prepared for court proceedings. Grasp of the children's history was not helped by frequent staff changes. The file may not even have been read before the hearing.* (Iwaniec et al., 2004)

Dickens (2004a) found that a major complaint of local authority lawyers was the amount of time they had to spend on overseeing the quality of social workers' written statements and reports. They were critical of standards of literacy, but their major concern was the proliferation of unnecessary detail and the inadequacy of analysis. One lawyer said:

> *It often just seems a diary of what they have done and that is it. I mean, they have got all that information and you cannot see in the statement how they have come to their conclusion.*

Duty of the court

Unless you are an independent social worker, it is unlikely that you will be asked to act as an expert witness in a formal sense. However, if you are giving evidence in a professional capacity, there is an important technical point. In litigation, witnesses make statements and experts write reports. Social workers are experts, and so what you write should follow the pattern of an expert's report, even though it may be called a statement.

Although the Civil Procedure Rules do not, for the most part, apply in family proceedings, Part 35 deals specifically with experts and assessors, and contains some important provisions. As a matter of good practice, we suggest that you treat these as applying to you as much as to any other expert. The most important is Part 35.3.

> (1) *It is the duty of an expert to help the court on the matters within his expertise.*

> (2) *This duty overrides any obligation to the person from whom he has received instructions, or by whom he is paid.*

This means that when giving evidence as an expert, you are not representing your employer and you are not there to support the case of one party over another. You are there to give your independent view, which means that in family cases you have a duty to include everything which might be relevant in deciding what is in the best interests of the child and to omit nothing. Separate rules apply to experts' reports in criminal proceedings (Part 33 of the Criminal Procedure Rules 2005).

Write your own statement

This may seem obvious, until you get into the clutches of lawyers. Because of their importance, in the interests of their clients lawyers are keen that reports and statements which are served on other parties before the trial or final hearing make the best possible impression. This can lead them to want to assist in their production, but there is a definite limit to what they may properly do. This limit is widely overstepped, at least in relation to the statements of witnesses of fact, which are often written by solicitors based on documents provided to them. Statements should be expressed in a witness's own words, and tell the whole story as perceived by them rather than an edited version of it. However, if you are not used to giving evidence, you may not appreciate what is relevant and what is not. Lawyers can offer guidance on what to include, but they should not suggest what you should say.

The Practice Direction to Part 35 of the Civil Procedure Rules states that:

> *1.2 Expert evidence should be the independent product of the expert, uninfluenced by the pressures of litigation.*

> *1.3 An expert should assist the court by providing objective, unbiased opinion on matters within his expertise, and should not assume the role of an advocate.*

> *1.4 An expert should consider all material facts, including those which might detract from his opinion.*

The Civil Justice Council (2005) has prepared a protocol, of which paragraph 15.2 is concerned with the influence which lawyers should, or rather should not, have on experts' reports:

> *Experts should not be asked to, and should not, amend, expand or alter any parts of reports in a manner which distorts their true opinion, but may be invited to amend or expand reports to ensure accuracy, internal consistency, completeness and relevance to the issues, and clarity. Although experts should generally follow the recommendations of solicitors with regard to the form of reports, they should form their own independent views as to the opinions and contents expressed in their reports, and exclude any suggestions which do not accord with their views.*

If you are asked if you have written your own statement, you must be able to answer with a confident *yes*, and stand by the statement in its entirety. If other people have made decisions in the case with which you do not agree, you must have the confidence to say so and explain why, otherwise you may face difficulties during cross-examination on your evidence.

> *I sometimes pick up a tension between the social worker and the line manager, who may well have a party line to follow. I wish that the actual social worker was able to state their own view, even if they then go on to say that the party line is different. (Family court judge)*

Preparation

For a busy practitioner, it is tempting to make use of summaries, reviews and other reports when reading up on the history of a case, but prior to writing a report which may have far-reaching consequences, you should read all of the case files and relevant documents. This may involve a great deal of work, particularly if the situation involves several family members, but it is essential to be fully informed before setting out your facts and opinion. As you are going to have to convey all this information to others, it is worth considering whether diagrams, such as ecomaps and genograms, would make it easier to explain a complex family situation. This kind of tool takes time to prepare and needs to be presented to a high standard to be effective.

It will help you maintain a balanced view if you have access to good quality supervision, or at least the opportunity seriously to consider possible alternative viewpoints. This can be difficult once legal proceedings are started but, as we have seen, it is important.

First steps

As in academic writing, it is important to prepare a plan, in consultation with your manager and legal adviser, so that you can be sure that nothing important is omitted. Similarly, you will need an introduction, followed by the main body of the report, and a balanced conclusion which summarises the main points. You should leave sufficient time to proof-read and edit what you have written before it is disclosed to the other parties, but you also need to ensure that it is completely up to date, which may mean adding material at the last minute. If you add anything, make sure that there is no repetition of what you wrote previously; if necessary, cross-refer instead. You will also have an opportunity to provide a verbal update at the beginning of any oral evidence.

As we have seen, ultimately everything which is relied on in court has to be shown to everyone involved, and although this should happen within formal court processes, it is normally good practice to try and ensure that your clients are prepared for what your report will contain. They may not agree with it, but at least they will have a little longer to consider its content than they otherwise would have done.

Setting out your report

The front sheet should include the name of the court, case number, names and dates of birth of the people covered by the report, the applicable legislation, your name, professional address and telephone number, and the date and number of the report. It should also be marked as confidential. You should then set out your qualifications and experience in order to establish your credentials; this is a requirement of a formal expert's report. The qualifications should be relevant to your practice as a social worker, starting with the highest, or most recent, first. It is not usual to include qualifications below university level, but if you have completed any relevant specialist training courses, include these together with the dates.

Next, describe your professional experience, which normally covers how long you have been a social worker, for whom you have worked and the type of work you have done. If you have relevant specialist experience or any publications or research to your name, these can be included. It is helpful to explain why you are writing your report, and if you are formally giving evidence as an expert, you must do so. At its simplest, you can state that you have been the social worker responsible for the case since a particular date and in what connection you are writing your report. Make it clear if you have been asked to address a specific issue.

What to include

In one sense, the title of this section would perhaps be better entitled *What not to include*. A common criticism of social work reports is that every single aspect of the case is included, which can result in important points being obscured by unnecessary detail. Obviously it is essential to include all relevant material, but a professional judgment needs to be made as to what this is. It is not likely to be necessary to give a detailed account of everything which has happened since the case first became known to your agency, and you should take account of other documents which will be put to the court, so that information is not duplicated. However, because it is so important, we repeat the fact that you must never omit relevant material which might be prejudicial to your own performance or the result you are hoping for. If you do, you will be particularly vulnerable during cross-examination and are likely to be criticised by the court.

CASE EXAMPLE

Re B [1994] 1 FCR 471

In this case, the social worker's evidence was criticised as being selective in the material taken from the case records, and the judge said:

I cannot emphasise too much that applicants such as a local authority responsible for children in their care ... should not act in a one hundred per cent adversarial way ... they must present [the case] in a balanced way and not fail to refer, it seems deliberately, to factors which point in a direction opposite to that which is desired by the local authority.

You should therefore spend time, and include your supervisor and legal adviser, on deciding what needs to be included. Frequently, legislation or guidance provides checklists or frameworks to define the scope of assessments, but your aim should always be to focus on and address the important issues in the case in a way which is fair and balanced and makes sense to all those involved. A pre-set agenda for the structure and content of reports is not usually as helpful to the court as it may be to you.

> *Social workers tend to follow a formula, and I can see that structure matters. In other words, nothing is left out. On the other hand, sometimes there is very little individual comment in the report. It is mostly the standard questions and answers, and it often looks far more substantial than it is.* (Family court judge)

It is usually sensible to start by explaining who everyone is. A genogram may help, but you also need to list anyone outside the family who is referred to in the report, for example, a teacher, health visitor, support worker or representative from a voluntary agency.

A chronology will provide the court with a list of key events and offers a useful overview, particularly at the start of any proceedings. Chronologies should be brief, contain no opinion or judgment, and identify essential facts which are accepted by all parties. They also need to be up to date.

Fact, analysis and opinion

When you are writing reports, whether they are for case files or specifically for court, try to look at them through the eyes of others, particularly those who might wish to challenge the facts or opinions you have recorded. It will also help you to improve the clarity of your expression if you take time to think about what a lawyer might make of what you have written. If cross-examined in court, how easy would you find it to explain what you meant? The next activity is designed to help you think about this.

ACTIVITY 7.1

You may be tempted to write of a client, X was angry. If it is suggested that they were not angry, how will you convince the court that your assessment was correct? You will find this easier if you support your opinion with evidence of fact:

> When I spoke to X, she replied in a raised voice, firmly and with conviction. She said that she was fed up with her partner, and was not going to waste any more time doing what he wanted.

What type of facts might be relevant to put forward to support the following opinions?

- *Jack is unwilling to find work.*

- *When Lisa is under pressure, she finds it hard to cope.*

- *There is concern about the lack of parental supervision.*

- *Thody's parents are worried about his behaviour.*

- *Mrs Sims is very dependent on the support of her partner.*

- *The relationship between the parents is extremely volatile.*

- *Amy is reluctant to accept help.*

We have heard social workers say that they have been told that they should stick to facts when writing records, and this is sometimes the framework for record-keeping undertaken by care and support workers. For student social workers, developing the knowledge, skills and confidence to express a professional opinion is one of the major challenges of their training. However, as we have seen, social workers are regarded by the courts as expert witnesses, and therefore in most situations they are expected to analyse the facts and use this to form professional opinions, just as other professional witnesses do. In fact, any reluctance to do so is likely to be picked up and may be regarded as lack of competence or credibility as a witness. However, a note of caution: when you express an opinion, you must only do so within the limits of your own expertise. This is particularly important in a case where evidence from other professionals would normally be sought before a conclusion is reached, as in a case of possible sexual abuse. If you have only worked on a very few cases in which sexual abuse was suspected, then your opinion will have to be far more tentative than if you have had many years' experience.

A professional opinion expressed in a report should always be based on analysis of material contained in that report. Everyone who reads it should be clear on what facts your opinion is based and to what extent you have personal knowledge of those facts. You should always give the source of any facts of which you do not have personal knowledge, such as case records made before you took over the case. If you are not the first person to have dealt with a case, it may be helpful to follow the summary of how the case was presented when you took it over with what you thought about it after you had got to know something about it and why you formed the view that you did. It is also a good idea to record that you have re-read your own case records to remind yourself of the details of your involvement. When referring to facts within your own knowledge, it is probably best to tell the story chronologically. There may be themes that you wish to cover separately, such as the involvement of a particular family member or the local authority's plans, but it is easier to follow a story if it is told in the order in which events happened.

In general you should avoid being dogmatic in expressing an opinion, unless you really believe that there is only one possible view. However, if there was no dispute about what should happen, it is not likely that there would be a court hearing. It is much more likely that there is a range of options for the court to consider and it is good practice to, and if you are instructed as an independent expert you must, describe the range of opinion on the issue in question.

Although the court needs to know what your opinion is, it is, if anything, more interested in how you formed this opinion. In other words, what facts did you take account of and how did you interpret and analyse them? The formulation of this rationale should, we suggest, incorporate four further Rs:

> ## *Rationale*
>
> **R**eading – *about any relevant theories; for example, attachment and loss.*
>
> **R**esearch – *into 'what works' in cases with factors which are similar to the one being tried; for example, how to ensure that an adoption placement of a child of a particular age has the best chance of success. However, if you refer to research, you must present a properly referenced and balanced overview (see below).*
>
> **R**esources – *what resources are needed and, more importantly, are available to support the plan proposed; for example, the realistic prospects of a specialist residential placement being available, and funded, within a reasonable period of time.*
>
> **R**eflection – *testing and analysing your thinking, so as to promote self-awareness and confidence in professional decision-making.*

If you have not got a reason for your opinion, you should not be expressing it. Sometimes, in highly technical cases, judges are allowed to get away with rather woolly reasons for their opinions; for example, a judge who has to choose between contrasting expert evidence may go for one opinion rather than another because the outcome seems fairer without being able to explain in sufficient detail to satisfy the respective experts what was wrong with the rejected evidence. Unfortunately, that soft option is not available to you. Courts are keenly interested in the reasons for your opinion and that of any other experts, and want to understand them so they can decide rationally on the right course to take.

You must make it clear if you do not feel you have all the relevant facts with which to form an opinion, and also if your opinion is based on disputed facts of which you have no personal knowledge and your opinion would be different if an alternative version of the facts was found to be correct. If you wish to qualify your opinion, you need to explain why. You also need to be able to explain and justify the process of analysis which led to the formation of your opinion. In most cases, your opinion will be based on your own knowledge and experience, which you will be able to describe, but if you wish to refer to research, it is wise to discuss it with your legal adviser. If you are going to rely wholly, or partly, on published research in justifying your opinion, you should clearly state this and attach the relevant article(s) to your report. You must also refer to any published material which you know about which does not support your view, attach copies and explain why your opinion is different. Again, if you do not do this, you risk being exposed in cross-examination or criticised by the court.

You should also consider whether any documents should be attached to your report, such as plans, letters or an agreement made with the family.

Point for reflection

This piece was written by a father who was involved in court proceedings under the Children Act 1989 which were to determine, among other things, the contact he was to have with his child, who did not live with him. The evidence considered by the court included a social worker's report, and the words not in italics are how the social worker interpreted what the father felt to be the true situation. It is unpublished, and was sent to lawyers as part of the father's campaign for more accountability and openness in family courts.

The wings of a butterfly

Did the child fall asleep in the car? overtired. *Did the father glance away from the child during an interview?* inattentive. *Was there a pause in the conversation between them?* little to say to each other. *Does the father play with the child?* over-enthusiastic. *Does he not play with the child?* lacking in enthusiasm. *Is the father anxious and apprehensive?* lacks interpersonal skills. *Does the father let the child play on the computer?* left to amuse himself unattended. *Does the father not let the child play on the computer?* withholds amenities. *Did the father smile?* makes light of the situation. *Has the father brought the child a present?* puts pressure on the child. *Did the child laugh and jump on the sofa?* allowed the child to become over-excited. *Did the child call the father 'Mr Silly' and try to pull his hair?* no clear boundaries. *Has the father bought some toys and other equipment?* trying to set up an alternative home. *Does the father miss the child?* emotionally needy. *Does the father desperately want to see more of the child?* unable to move forward. *Did the father say he wants to see the child because he loves him?* confuses his own needs with those of the child. *Does the father disagree with the social worker?* inflexible. *Does the father refuse to agree that his medical records be produced?* failing to demonstrate an ability to prioritise the welfare of the child.

This piece offers a powerful illustration of how a social worker's analysis of a fairly straightforward series of events was completely at odds with that of the subject of the report. It may help you interpret more accurately if you consider how you might feel if the report in question had been written about you.

Use of language

One of the most important aspects of presenting evidence, whether written or spoken, is use of language. Language should be a means, and not a barrier, to communication and a report which uses language which is vague, confusing, lacks rigour and contains jargon, acronyms or clichés is likely to land you in considerable difficulty, particularly when being cross-examined. Judges also cherish brevity and clarity (Bond and Sandhu, 2005). For some reason, social workers do not have a particularly good reputation when it comes to use of language. They seem inclined to take ordinary words and phrases and surround them with a mystique which leads to barriers to understanding and can be a gift to the cross-examining lawyer. This is illustrated by the following story, which was told to us by a student social worker who observed the event on placement.

CASE EXAMPLE

While visiting a man to assess his need for community care services, the social worker explained to him that the aim of the resulting care plan was to empower him, to which he replied: That's very kind of you, but I don't need to be empowered as I've just signed up with British Gas.

Other examples are the service user who said she thought that the phrase *case conference* meant that everyone attending the meeting would be carrying a briefcase and another who thought that *eligibility criteria* had something to do with joining a dating agency. We once observed a social worker struggling to explain to a judge what the description *key-worker* meant. When she finished, the judge observed drily, *I see; so it has nothing to do with keys then?* Not, perhaps, a major error, but it does not inspire confidence in social workers' ability to express themselves clearly and concisely, or make their comments easily understood. It can also make service users feel excluded and confused at a time when they are facing many unfamiliar and often frightening experiences.

I would like the social worker to tell me in plain English what they really think. Far better to say that they found the mother fed-up and difficult, *and describe the facts which led to this conclusion, than some bromide expression like* Mrs Smith's co-operation was a little lacking.

Behavioural problems *could mean anything from a tendency to fidget to a propensity to arson.*

Kevin has difficulty relating adequately to his peer group *just means he hasn't got any friends.*

(Family court judges)

Lawyers can sometimes appear to non-lawyers to be overly concerned with use of language. However, a substantial part of their work involves determining the meaning of specific words or phrases. Unclear language in a will, lease or contract of employment, for example, can result in disputes which require a considerable amount of unravelling (as in the proverbial will which contained only the words *All To Mother*). It follows, then, that any ambiguity or lack of clarity in reports or evidence is likely to attract the court's attention. In fact, there is really no excuse for using language which is likely to lead to misunderstanding, confusion or exclusion, either in or out of court. It would do so much for both social worker/lawyer and social worker/client relations if social workers were to express themselves clearly, concisely and, above all, simply.

ACTIVITY 7.2

In relation to the following expressions, see if you can find a single word that would do just as well:

- *on a regular basis;*

- *arrive at a conclusion;*

- *as a matter of course;*

- *fail to recognise;*

- *is of the opinion that;*

- *have been identified as being.*

In almost every situation, it is preferable to use as the minimum number of words necessary to convey the message.

AVOID JARGON LIKE THE PLAGUE
(Family court judge)

The next examples are designed to help you think about what language you use and devise ways to improve your expression. It is impossible to over-emphasise the importance of this in the court setting. The first concerns the use of jargon. Jargon is a form of shorthand in which pseudo-technical vocabulary is used to make things sound more important (as in *sibling* instead of *brother* or *sister*). It is also a way of repackaging ordinary events to fit within particular professional categories or theories. What it actually does is create barriers, emphasise power differentials and make it difficult or impossible for those who are not in on the secret to understand what is meant.

Once you have got into the habit of using jargon, it is very difficult to stop. It is something of a mystery to us why social workers are so prone to using jargon. It might have something to do with lack of professional confidence, or it may be picked up from the style of language now used in many official communications. Sometimes it represents an attempt to obscure the reality of a situation, or to remove potentially negative connotations (as in *challenging behaviour* or *mental health issues*).

Whatever the reason for its use, it does not accord with basic social work values. If what you say or write cannot be easily understood by other professionals or, even more importantly, service users whose interests should be central to your practice, then you are not meeting basic professional standards. Having said this, we have to acknowledge that lawyers are certainly not blameless in this respect. Some of the most commonly used legal terms are described in Chapter 4. If you come across legal expressions or acronyms that you don't understand, you should not hesitate to ask for clarification. You might also reflect on how it feels to be excluded in this way.

tionships in the future. This is particularly important in the context of what one party may have said about or done to another, or when dealing with an issue on which there are strongly opposing views.

Presentation

Anyone involved in court proceedings has to assimilate a huge amount of written material. As first impressions are influential, it follows that anything which is poorly presented will stand out and may result in a negative judgment of its writer which is hard to reverse. Hopefully, it goes without saying that reports should be free of grammatical and spelling errors. Numbered pages and paragraphs, each of which should refer to one main point, make it easier to refer to specific sections, and many courts request wide margins and double line spacing, so that notes can be added. In essays, students are usually advised that sub-headings impede the flow, but in a long report they can be useful signposts, particularly if they are numbered and indexed at the beginning. Any additional material included should be listed so that the whole document is easy to navigate.

Statement of truth

Witness statements made in proceedings to which the Civil Procedure Rules apply must contain what is called a statement of truth: *I believe the facts stated in this witness statement are true*. This may seem simply a formality, but making a false statement verified by a statement of truth, without an honest belief in the truth of the statement is contempt of court. You should therefore take great care that everything in your statement is accurate before signing a statement of truth.

Additional requirements for formal experts' reports

A formal expert's report is addressed to the court, not the party which has commissioned it. In addition to the matters already considered, it must contain a summary of conclusions, a formal statement that you understand your duty to the court and that you have complied with it, and a statement of truth, the wording of which is slightly different from that attached to an ordinary witness statement: *I confirm that insofar as the facts stated in my report are within my own knowledge I have made clear which they are and I believe them to be true, and that the opinions I have expressed represent my true and complete professional opinion.*

Probation and youth justice reports

Reports prepared by probation and youth offending teams are, of course, experts' reports but prepared in a special context to comply with Home Office National Standards for the Supervision of Offenders in the Community 2000 or the National Standards for Youth Justice Services 2004. Probation National Standards allow little scope for initiative as the content and layout of each type of report is clearly prescribed. One of the disadvantages of this, as with assessment frameworks and other types of checklist, is that you may concentrate on covering all the required factual issues at the expense of expressing a clearly argued professional opinion.

It is interesting that probation National Standards appear to contemplate slightly different approaches to different types of report: a bail information report should be *objective, factual and impartial*, while a pre-sentence report is to be *objective, impartial, free from discriminatory language and stereotype, balanced, verified and factually accurate*, and a specific sentence report is not required to have any of these qualities. However, we think it is clear that probation and youth justice reports should comply with the standards of witness statements and reports discussed in this chapter.

A final word

If you are writing a statement or report, all you can really do is tell the story as you perceived it, as fully as you can. However, if you are offering professional analysis and opinion, you want the court to take notice of it. We have read many witness statements and experts' reports which can run to tens, or even hundreds, of pages and require a high level of concentration and dedication on the part of the reader. You are more likely to make an impact if what you have written is well set out, clearly signposted, structured, focused and interesting. You don't want the readers wondering whether you are ever going to get to the point.

C H A P T E R   S U M M A R Y

In the court setting, reports and statements are the primary means by which social work practice is exposed to scrutiny, and for service users they represent professional power at its most daunting. As with any aspect of court work, preparation is the key to writing reports which are relevant, comprehensive, balanced, focused and well-presented. It is important to continue to develop your skills in use of language, by reading widely and regularly analysing the effectiveness of written material.

FURTHER READING

Cooper, P. (2006) *Reporting to the Court under the Children Act*, 2nd edn. London: Stationery Office. This contains advice, examples and checklists to help those preparing local authority statements and reports.

Hopkins, G. (1998a) *Plain English for Social Services: A Guide to Better Communication*. Lyme Regis: Russell House.

Hopkins, G. (1998b) *The Write stuff: A Guide to Effective Writing in Social Care and Related Services*. Lyme Regis: Russell House.
Both are entertaining books which offer guidance, supported by examples, on how to communicate effectively in writing.

NACRO (2003) *Pre-sentence Reports for Young People: A Good Practice Guide*, 2nd edn. London: NACRO.

WEBSITES

www.writeenough.org.uk

This interactive training pack, commissioned by the Children's Services Division of the Department of Health (now the Department for Education and Skills) supports good practice in recording. It explains, and gives examples of, key child and family records, including chronologies, genograms, care, adoption and pathway plans.

www.ewi.org.uk

The Expert Witness Institute website provides a template for expert witness reports.

www.nationalarchives.gov.uk

The National Archives website contains information on National Standards for the Supervision of Offenders in the Community 2000.

www.scie.org.uk/elearning/index.asp

Contains an interactive courtroom case study, based on social work reports.

www.yjb.gov.uk

Standard 7 of National Standards for Youth Justice Services relates to reports for courts and youth offender panels.

Chapter 8

What to expect at court

Introduction

Unless you are an experienced witness, it helps to become acclimatised to the court and to the people in it before you give evidence.

- What does a courtroom look like?

- In what order are things likely to happen?

- How formal are the proceedings?

- Will everything you say be recorded?

- Will your evidence be all over the newspapers?

Having answers to these questions will help you feel more confident when you come to give your evidence.

What does a court look like?

Hearings in open court

You probably have an idea what a courtroom looks like from films or television. At the front of the court room is the bench, a long desk where the judge sits, facing everyone else. In

Victorian courts, the bench may be as much as six feet higher than the rest of the room, but in modern courts it is usually only a couple of feet higher. The judge's entrance is behind or beside the bench, in front of which, to one side, is the witness box. In front of the bench is a long table where the clerk, and perhaps an usher, sits, behind which are tables for the lawyers. In modern courts the front row is for QCs, if there are any, the next is for junior barristers and behind them sit solicitors. QCs do not usually appear in County or magistrates' courts, so these courts usually have two rows of tables (see Figures 8.1 and 8.2). In criminal courts the dock is likely to be opposite the witness box, with a separate entrance from the cells below. In Crown Courts the jury sits in two rows of seats to one side of the court, with a desk in front. There are usually seats reserved for the press, and in criminal courts, for probation and police liaison officers. In civil courts the claimant's lawyers usually sit on the left and the defendant's lawyers sit on the right, as you face the judge. In the Crown Court, the prosecution lawyer is furthest away from the jury, with the defendant's lawyer nearest the jury.

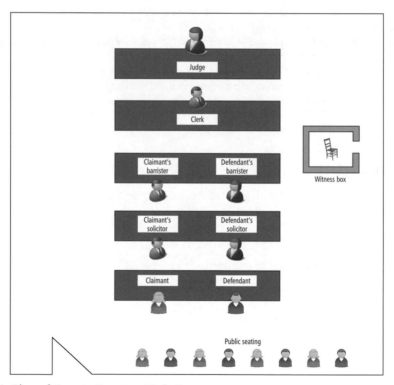

Figure 8.1 Plan of County Court or High Court

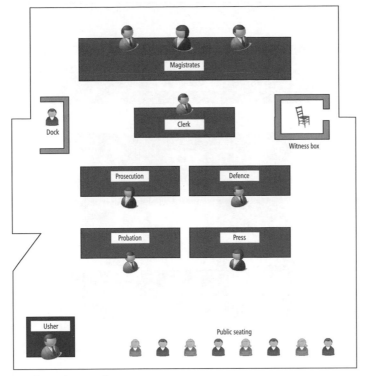

Figure 8.2 Plan of Magistrates' court

Private hearings in the County or High Court

Private County Court hearings are usually held in a room like an office. The judge sits at a desk, with a conference table in front for the lawyers and anyone else involved in the case. Some County Court hearings, and private hearings in the High Court, take place in an ordinary court room from which the press and public are excluded.

Family courts

The layout of a magistrates' court sitting as a family court is similar to that of a County Court district judge's room (see Figure 8.3).

Youth courts

Magistrates' youth courts are arranged differently from other criminal courts to try to make them less intimidating for young people (see Figure 8.4). Although the public is excluded, the press may attend, although no identifying details of the child or young person concerned can be published.

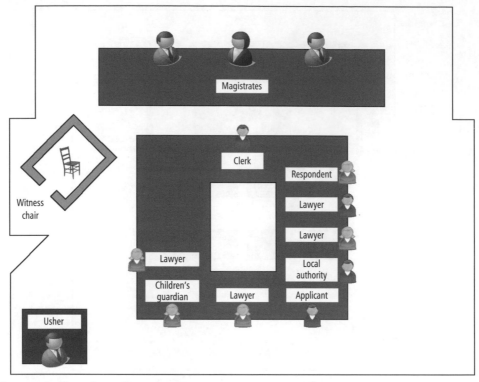

Figure 8.3 Plan of Family Proceedings Court

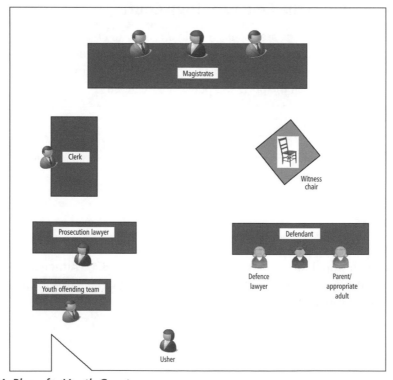

Figure 8.4 Plan of a Youth Court

What do judges wear?

Judges never wear in court the elaborate ceremonial robes seen on formal occasions, so you will never see them in long wigs, breeches and stockings, except on television. Until recently, court business was either conducted in open court or *in chambers*, which was essentially the judge's room. Most of the business conducted in chambers was not actually private, although the size of the room meant that not many people could attend. The modern tendency is to distinguish between business which is truly private, such as family matters, and that to which the public and press should have access in the interests of justice. Hearings which used to be held in chambers, but which are not private, are now held *unrobed*, except in the Family Division, where the old form of words is still used. In unrobed hearings, the judges and lawyers wear ordinary suits. Formal hearings, such as trials, in which judges and lawyers wear robes, are described as *robed*.

District judges almost always sit unrobed, as do Masters and Registrars.

Recorders and Deputy High Court judges who are barristers wear the robes they wear when appearing in court normally.

Circuit judges wear violet robes, rather like dressing gowns, over ordinary clothes, a short judge's wig and, if male, bands and a wing collar. Over the left shoulder is a sash, which is red in the Crown Court and lilac in the County Court.

Circuit judges sitting as High Court judges, High Court judges in the Chancery and Family Division and Appeal Court judges all wear the same as a QC, except that the wig is a judge's wig, which is close fitting and has no curls. Barrister's wigs have curls and are quite loose.

Queen's Bench Division judges wear red robes in criminal cases, with fur facings in the winter and silk facings in the summer, black robes in winter civil trials and blue/violet robes in summer, both with a scarlet sash.

House of Lords judges only ever wear lounge suits.

There has been consultation in respect of whether judges should continue to wear robes in court, and it is likely that judges hearing civil cases will stop wearing wigs, collars and bands from October 2007.

What do lawyers wear?

- Junior barristers' court dress is a black gathered gown, wig and, if male, a wing collar and bands, worn over an ordinary suit.

- QCs wear a black tail coat and waistcoat, over trousers or a skirt, or a sleeved waistcoat, which has no tails and is more practical and comfortable. They wear the same wig, collar and bands as junior barristers, but their gown is not gathered and originally, at least, was made of silk, which is why being appointed a QC is sometimes referred to as *taking silk*. Most QCs now wear a rayon gown, which is cheaper and more hard-wearing.

- When robed, solicitors wear bands and a wing collar, if male, and a black gown which is different from either of the barristers' gowns.

ACTIVITY 8.1

What advantages and disadvantages do you see in lawyers and judges wearing robes, from the point of view of the users of courts (litigants, witnesses, people facing criminal charges, jurors, experts, other professionals, lawyers, judges)?

When reflecting on this activity, you might like to think about your reaction to other situations in which people wear uniforms: hospitals, police stations, care homes, schools, airports, churches.

A barrister's view on wearing wigs (letter to the Daily Telegraph, *15 January 2007):*

> *Wigs disguise judges and have the additional benefit of obscuring how decrepit they are. I sat as a deputy judge to enforce a maintenance order, substantially in arrears. For this purpose, I had to wear my wig. The delinquent husband was not pleased with my order and for months afterwards mounted a one-man picket outside the Royal Courts of Justice bearing a placard that stated his opinion of me in no uncertain terms. On many days when doing my day job as a barrister, I had to pass right in front of him in order to get into the building. He did not recognise me once.*

How do you address a judge?

Bearing in mind how many different types of judge there are, this is reassuringly simple. At all levels below recorder, and in magistrates' courts and tribunals, use *Sir* or *Madam*. Recorders and circuit judges are addressed as *Your Honour* and High Court judges, Appeal Court judges and judges in the House of Lords are all *My Lord* or *My Lady*.

What do you do when you get to court?

This depends on why you are there. In particular it depends on whether you have to be available to discuss the case with lawyers or only to give evidence. In most cases, social workers have to do both.

Pre-trial conference or consultation

On the first day of a hearing, there is usually a conference or consultation before the hearing starts. The lawyers may have some last-minute thoughts to discuss with you, or there may have been developments which they need to know about. We suggest that you should be at court at least half an hour before the hearing is due to start, although earlier may be suggested.

Negotiations

In ordinary civil litigation the emphasis is on settling the case if at all possible, but it is often only on the day of the hearing that any of the parties turn their minds sensibly to the possibilities of settlement, which may have something to do with recognising the risks of failure. In family cases involving children, a settlement is not achievable by the parties alone, as the approval of the court is needed, which may mean that it is not until the hearing approaches that anyone, including the lawyers, gives serious thought to the possibilities of compromise. You should therefore allow time for any negotiations before the hearing begins. If you are the case social worker, your participation in these, at least at the level of being able to discuss proposals with the lawyers, is essential. You may also find that the court agrees to delay the hearing so that further discussions can take place. However, these kinds of negotiations can pose difficulties for social workers.

> *Lawyers – and to some extent guardians – seem happy to conduct the majority of their business at court. Social workers and their managers are often put under pressure to negotiate or make decisions which they either do not have authority to make, or which require resources which they are not able to guarantee are available.* (Child protection team manager)

It is important that the lawyers understand the decision-making process in your agency, and you should try to ensure that a responsible manager is with you in court, at least for the start and expected end of the hearing.

Confidentiality

A common practical problem is how to maintain confidentiality. Courts do not usually have much interview space, and it is not uncommon for discussions to take place in corridors or other public areas. If possible, you should insist that people's private affairs are not discussed in places where they can be overheard. If it is anticipated that there will not be a room available at the court, then other arrangements need to be planned for any discussions.

Attending the hearing

Lawyers want someone who can react to what is happening to be in court throughout the hearing. In particular they need someone who can comment on what is being said on behalf of another party. If you are the case social worker, you are best equipped to do this, and so you should expect to attend the whole of every day of the hearing. If you are instructed as an independent expert, you will probably have to attend court during any factual evidence relevant to opinions you have expressed. If anything emerges which causes you to change or modify your opinion, you must tell the lawyers who have asked you to be involved in the case. You should also do this if you are the case social worker and wish to alter any opinion expressed in your witness statement. You will almost certainly, either as an independent expert or the case social worker, be asked to comment on any expert evidence called on behalf of other parties and to suggest possible lines of questioning. If you are an independent expert, it does not compromise your independence to inform your client's lawyer of any fallacies you see in another expert's opinion. However, you are not an advocate for your client, and professional embarrassment of another expert is not a proper aim, however tempting it may be.

The atmosphere in court

All court proceedings are fairly formal, although magistrates' courts tend to be less so than higher courts. However, the degree of formality can be a barrier if you are not familiar with it.

ACTIVITY **8.2**

In relation to a decision-making forum with which you have been involved, assess how far the degree of formality influenced the following essential aspects:

- *adhering to a clear agenda;*

- *ensuring that everyone had a chance to contribute effectively;*

- *keeping the discussion focused on the task;*

- *providing the opportunity for negotiation;*

- *dealing with conflict;*

- *keeping within a reasonable time limit;*

- *reaching a decision;*

- *clarifying the means by which the decision would be implemented and evaluated.*

What does this tell you about the value, or otherwise, of formality in court proceedings?

This exercise encourages you to compare and contrast formality in court proceedings with more familiar decision-making arenas, and to identify positive aspects of formality to counterbalance the more obvious negative ones.

Whether to bow

At the start of a hearing or on entering court, everyone used to be expected to bow towards the judge or magistrates as a mark of respect. You will see that lawyers and court staff still do this, although often it is little more than a brief nod of the head. Increasingly, in civil courts parties and witnesses are not expected to bow, although it is still common in criminal courts.

Humour

Occasionally court proceedings have their lighter moments. Some cases which revolve around rather dry questions of commercial law can be quite boring, even for the paid participants. There is a game which barristers used to play, in which the challenge was to use a word chosen by colleagues without the judge recognising the alien concept. One of us once successfully introduced the word *hippopotamus* into a case about wheat farming in Norfolk, and if the judge noticed, he was not brave enough to say. Most humour is unintended, however. When judges were less familiar with popular culture, they sometimes caused amusement by asking questions like *Who are the Beatles?* or, in a case in which one of us was involved, *What is a twin-tub washing machine?* However, most judges today are reasonably in touch with ordinary life and fortunately such embarrassing remarks are rare.

In some proceedings, especially those involving children, the judge and lawyers usually try to make the hearing less intimidating. However, you should take your lead from them. In discussions with other professionals during adjournments, to relieve tension it is sometimes tempting to adopt a familiar or even humorous tone, but you should never lose sight of the fact that there is likely to be a great deal at stake for some of the people involved, and observing too much informality among professionals can cause them confusion or distress.

> *In court, parents often get the impression that the social workers are very chummy with the lawyers, and that all the professionals are in cahoots with each other, which can be very bewildering and upsetting.* (Parents' Aid representative)

In what order do things happen?

All court hearings follow essentially the same pattern. There are basically two types of hearing:

- hearings in anticipation of a trial; and

- the formal trial.

Pre-trial hearings may be the result of a court order that there should be a hearing, or because one of the parties has made an application. Case management conferences, directions hearings and pre-trial reviews are all intended to ensure that the case proceeds smoothly and with as little delay as possible. Not every case will have all of these types of hearing, and usually they will be managed by the lawyers. However, it is never possible to predict exactly what will happen, and preparation is the key:

> *So I walk into court, sitting there thinking 'oh my God, I hope they don't ask me any questions' and I was just told 'it's a directions hearing, just go there, sit down and you don't have to say anything', and then I went in and there were all these questions.*

(Social worker, quoted by Dickens, 2004b)

Any hearing or trial begins by being called on. For private hearings this simply involves the usher saying that the judge is ready to deal with the case. In open court hearings, the clerk or usher announces the case, which alerts everyone that it is about to begin, and records the name of the case on the tape recording made of most hearings in open court. The lawyer for the party who started the proceedings then introduces the other lawyers, and what happens next depends on whether the hearing is of an application or is a trial.

Applications

An application can be made by any party. In civil and family cases, the lawyers usually deliver to court in advance skeleton arguments, which set out what the application is about, a summary of the evidence and what arguments are relied on to support or oppose it. The judge reads the skeleton arguments before the hearing and may also read the case papers. Sets of the relevant papers are usually copied and assembled in files, called bundles. Pages are numbered and each bundle has a letter or number. Often dividers, known as tabs, are inserted to mark sections with documents of a particular type, like previous court orders. You may therefore hear references to bundle A tab 3, and so on. Bundles are usually sent to court in advance by post or courier. There is a good chance that they will arrive crushed, with the rings out of alignment, which provides considerable scope for displays of judicial dissatisfaction. Another potential source of difficulty is bundles being numbered differently, particularly if the judge's bundles have different page numbers from everybody else's, or pages have been added after a hearing has started and someone's bundle has been left out of the process.

Applications proceed as follows, unless they are being made without notice and the respondent does not attend, which could happen, for example, in relation to an application for an emergency protection order under s. 44 of the Children Act 1989.

- *Applicant's lawyer opens the application* by explaining what it is about and referring to evidence relied on in support of it and any evidence in opposition. As the hearing is not a trial, the evidence consists only of written witness statements and any documents attached. The lawyer then puts forward arguments as to why the application should be granted. If the application is a case management conference or a pre-trial review, it is opened by the claimant's lawyer (or prosecution in a criminal case), who explains what the case is about. It is unlikely that there will be any evidence, as the focus of attention will probably be practical matters.

- *Lawyers for opposing parties put arguments to the court* Conventionally the respondents' arguments are put by the first respondent, followed by the second respondent and so on, although sometimes groups of respondents use the same lawyer. If some respondents support the application and some oppose it, supporting arguments are heard before the opposing ones.

- *Applicant's lawyer closes the application* by responding to the arguments against it.

- *Judge's decision*.

Civil trials

The case papers at trials are assembled in the same way as for applications, and they proceed as follows:

- *Introduction of the lawyers*

- *Claimant's lawyer explains what the case is about (opens the case)* Skeleton arguments are the rule, and the judge reads the case papers before the trial starts. Consequently, the opening of the case may be quite short. However, the lawyer may read out, or ask the judge to read, further documents which can take hours or even days if the case is complex.

- *Claimant's witnesses give oral evidence* If witness statements are not disputed they are taken as read and witnesses need only attend court if the lawyer for another party wishes to question them. The first witness is usually the claimant. There usually follow other witnesses of fact, and then any expert witnesses. However, the order can be adapted to accommodate witnesses with other commitments and to avoid keeping people waiting to give evidence. As we have seen, evidence in chief of witnesses in civil trials is given in writing. The lawyer for the party calling a witness may ask the judge's permission to ask additional questions, but this is only agreed if there is a valid reason, such as the fact that something in another witness statement needs to be answered and is not covered in the witness's existing statement. If there are no supplementary questions, witnesses are invited to look at their witness statements, and asked whether they have read them recently and whether the contents are true.

- *Cross-examination of claimant's witnesses by lawyers for the other parties* Each witness is cross-examined after verifying their witness statement. This usually takes place in the order in which the parties are listed in the court documents, which is claimant, followed by defendants first to last. This order may be adjusted so that cross-examination by lawyers for parties sympathetic to the case of the party calling the witness takes place before cross-examination by parties hostile to the case. This is so that *friendly* cross-examination cannot try to undo any damage done previously by *hostile* cross-examination.

- *Re-examination by claimant's lawyer* This is a chance to clarify evidence which may have been based on misunderstanding a question, or not being shown a relevant document. However, it can weaken the evidence from the point of view of the party calling the witness, partly because, if the evidence which the lawyer thinks is damaging is the witness's true evidence, seeking to undo it, but having it confirmed, just draws attention to it. Also, after cross-examination witnesses tend to relax when facing their own lawyer, which can produce a lapse in concentration, a failure to listen to questions properly and, possibly, unfortunate admissions.

- *Claimant's lawyer closes case*. After this, claimants cannot call further evidence without the court's permission.

- *Defendant's evidence*. Defendants can insist that all the claimant's evidence is heard before any evidence is given on their behalf, because they do not have to call any evidence at all, even if they have served witness statements. However, if a statement or expert's report is served without its author giving evidence, another party can rely on the statement or report as evidence. Unless a defendant is preserving the option not to call evidence, in cases with a strong technical element, the factual evidence is sometimes heard before expert evidence, which is sensible if none of the experts knows the facts of the case and there is a serious dispute about them. If the factual evidence is heard first, the experts can take account of this.

- *Cross-examination by other defendants' lawyers, if there are any*

- *Cross-examination by claimant's lawyer* who can rely on any favourable answers in support of their case.

- *Re-examination by defendant's lawyer*

- *Defendant's lawyer closes their case*

- *Closing speeches* are usually made in reverse order to the listing on the formal court documents, so the claimant's lawyer usually has the last word. However, if a defendant has called no evidence, their lawyer is entitled to make the last speech. In closing speeches lawyers make submissions, which means advancing arguments as to what evidence the judge should accept, what the relevant law is and how it should be applied to the facts of the case.

- *The judge's decision* not only involves deciding who has won, but also what findings of fact to make, determining, if disputed, the relevant law and applying it to the facts which are found proved. The formal judgment sets out the judge's findings and the reasons for them. Depending upon the length and complexity of the trial, judgment may be given orally at once (called *ex tempore*, Latin for *at the time*) or later, called reserving judgment. Unless the delay is no longer than overnight, a reserved judgment is almost always in writing. Written judgments are not read out in court, but are provided to the lawyers in advance. They must not tell anyone the result until one hour before the judgment is given formally, a process called *handing down*. Then there are arguments about costs and a formal order, also called, confusingly, a judgment, is prepared to give effect to the decision.

Trials in family cases

These are similar to other civil trials and are usually called final hearings. The lawyers open their case and evidence is called in the same way. The order of proceedings under the Children Act 1989 is determined by Rule 4.21 of the Family Proceedings Rules 1991. Each party explains its case, and calls evidence in the following order:

- applicant;
- anyone with parental responsibility;

- other respondents;

- children's guardian;

- child, if a party to the proceedings and there is no children's guardian.

Criminal trials

In Crown Courts defendants usually admit or deny (*plead to*) each charge (*count*) in the list of charges (*indictment*) against them at a Plea and Case Management Hearing, when arrangements are also made for the trial, if there is a *not guilty* plea to any charge. In Crown Courts, if a defendant is asked how they plead at the start of what is supposed to be the trial, it is probably because they are changing a previous plea from *not guilty* to *guilty*. In magistrates' courts pleas are entered before or at the start of the trial.

Criminal trials are conducted rather differently from civil ones:

- *Start of trial* The court is told whether the defendant has admitted or not admitted any of the charges. In magistrates' courts there is no jury, and the trial starts once it is clear what charges the defendant faces.

- *Crown Court jury is sworn in (empanelled)* A group of about 15 people is brought into court. Their names are written on cards which are shuffled by the court clerk, who calls them out in order from the top, after which those named go to sit in the jury box. Anyone who knows the defendant, or someone connected with the case, is excused, which is why the number of people brought into court is more than the twelve required. Any objection to a potential juror is dealt with as they come to take the oath *faithfully to try the defendant and to give a true verdict according to the evidence*. Lawyers and judges used to be prohibited from serving on juries, but since exemptions were lifted in 2004, jury summoning officers have had a lot of fun calling judges to serve on juries.

Alternative types of criminal trial.

- **France** *In serious criminal cases, a jury of nine retires with the three judges and all twelve decide together on the defendant's guilt and the sentence to be applied.*

- **Germany** *There is no jury and guilt or innocence is decided by a single judge or a judge sitting with two lay (unqualified) judges.*

- **Spain** *A jury of nine lay people have to give reasons for their decisions.*

- **Scotland** *The jury numbers 15, and there is a third verdict, in addition to* guilty *and* not guilty, *of not proven, which is similar in effect to a verdict of* not guilty *but shows that the jury was not particularly impressed by the defence case.*

- **United States of America** *In states where there is a death penalty, a jury decides in capital cases whether it should be imposed.*

- **France, Spain and Russia** *The jury is asked to provide answers to questions formulated by the judge as steps leading to the final decision as to whether the defendant is guilty – in other words, they have to show how they have reached their verdict.*

ACTIVITY 8.3

Juries' discussions while considering their verdicts are secret and they are not required to give reasons for their decisions. Also, juries have no role in relation to sentencing if they find someone guilty.

- *Do you think that this is compatible with Article 6 of the European Convention on Human Rights (right to a fair trial)?*

- *List the advantages and disadvantages that you can see in the present jury system.*

- *Do you think a jury trial is a fair method of determining guilt?*

- *What alternative system could you suggest?*

- *Do you think that juries should have a role in determining sentences?*

The activity encourages you to think critically about systems and procedures which are found in criminal courts, particularly from the point of view of defendants.

- *Prosecution opens its case* The jury is told what charges the defendant faces and is shown the indictment, but is unlikely to know if the defendant has admitted any charge unless the defendant requests it. For example, a defendant who admits having killed someone, but denies that it was intended, may admit manslaughter, but deny murder. By long-hallowed economy jurors do not each get a copy of the indictment, it is one between two. The burden of proving guilt of a criminal charge is on the prosecution, which describes the charges against the defendant and the evidence to be called to support them. In Crown Courts, and in limited types of cases in magistrates' courts, defendants have to tell the prosecution what their defence is, but do not have to disclose the evidence on which they intend to rely.

- *Prosecution calls its evidence* Unlike in civil proceedings, evidence in chief is given orally prompted by questions, and leading questions are not permitted. Witnesses therefore have to try to remember what is in their statement, which is particularly challenging if the incident in question occurred some time previously. During the prosecution evidence the jury may be asked to retire for the judge to make a ruling of law. Often the issue relates to the admissibility of evidence under the technical rules which apply in criminal cases. In civil cases more or less any evidence is admissible and it is up to the judge to decide what it is worth, but in criminal cases the rules are intended to ensure that the jury only hears evidence which, if they believe it, would be reliable evidence on which to base a conviction.

- *Cross-examination of prosecution witnesses by defence lawyers* Each of them has a copy of the witness's statement, although the witness does not. Each witness is cross-examined immediately after giving evidence in chief. Defendants who are not legally represented can personally cross-examine prosecution witnesses in most cases.

- *Re-examination by prosecution*

- *Possible submission by defence* At this point the defendant's lawyers can make a submission to the judge or magistrates that the prosecution has not proved its case, even if the defendant calls no evidence (*discloses no case to answer*). If the submission is accepted, the jury is directed to return a *not guilty* verdict. Submissions take place in the jury's absence, so that they are not influenced if the judge rejects them, but magistrates are supposed to be able to proceed with the trial uninfluenced by an unsuccessful submission of no case to answer.

- *Evidence from defendant* If the trial is not ended by a successful submission of no case to answer, defendants have to decide whether to give evidence themselves. If they choose not to, it will be the subject of comment by the judge before the jury considers its verdict and is also taken into account by magistrates in reaching a decision. A defendant who gives evidence is the first of the defence witnesses to be called. Defendants' evidence is given in the same way as prosecution evidence, by question and answer. The prosecution does not have statements from defendants or their witnesses, and so does not usually know what they are likely to say. Defendants with no previous convictions are entitled to call evidence of their good character.

- *Cross-examination of defendant's witnesses* Cross-examination of defence witnesses is by lawyers for any other defendants in the order on the indictment and then by the prosecution.

- *Re-examination by defendant's lawyer*

- *Prosecution makes submissions* as to what evidence should be accepted and the law which, on the facts put forward, means that the defendant is guilty of the alleged charges.

- *Defendant's lawyer makes submissions* Defendants' lawyers do not have to try to persuade the jury or the magistrates that their client is innocent, but concentrate on emphasising doubts that they are guilty. They may also make submissions as to which witnesses should be believed and, possibly, as to the relevant law.

- *Judge's summing up* In Crown Courts the judge reminds the jury that he deals with questions of law and they decide the facts. The jury is then instructed on the law which they must apply to the facts, known as *directions to the jury*. The judge also reminds the jury of the evidence which the judge thinks is important, but this is not binding on jurors, who can make their own decisions about both evidence and facts.

- *Court considers its verdict* Most judges do not send a jury out to consider a verdict after about 3 p.m. They adjourn the case and leave about five minutes' worth of summing up for the following morning. If the jury reaches unanimous agreement, they return to announce their verdict. If they cannot agree within about two and a quarter hours, the judge asks whether they are likely to be able to reach a unanimous verdict, in which case they can continue their deliberations. If they suggest this is unlikely, the judge tells them that a verdict on which at least ten of them agree can be accepted, and they continue their discussions which, in long and complex cases, can go on for days. However, usually, after a few hours the judge says that the court will take any verdicts which have been agreed, and discharges the jury from reaching verdicts on any counts on which they cannot agree. If guilty verdicts are returned, the question of sentence arises. After the speeches for the defendants, magistrates decide whether the case against them has been proved.

- *Sentencing* There are restrictions on courts imposing a term of imprisonment without first obtaining a pre-sentence report from the probation or youth offending service. Whether a community sentence is appropriate is also a decision which can usually only be made after the court knows what is available. Consequently, after a *guilty* verdict most cases are adjourned for reports. The sentencing part of a hearing follows much the same format, whether or not it has been adjourned previously. The prosecution details the defendant's criminal record, if there is one. If it is long, the court may ask that only the last so-many offences, or a summary, are given. If the defendant has no previous convictions, details of their family circumstances and employment are given. The defendant's lawyer then makes a *plea in mitigation*, a speech about the appropriate punishment which takes account of information or recommendations in any reports and any previous convictions. More details of the defendant's circumstances and plans are usually given, together with expressions of remorse, unless this is totally implausible. The judge or magistrates announce the sentence and explain aspects of the sentencing decision and its effects. In serious cases, where a sentence of imprisonment is being imposed, reference to protection of the public and the impact on any victim may be included.

Recording the proceedings

In all courts someone records what is said, even if it is only the judge in a notebook. These notes are for the judge's own use and, as it is unlikely that the judge has shorthand skills, they will not be verbatim notes. In civil and family proceedings, because the evidence in chief is in writing, the judge notes the important parts of the evidence which supplement the witness statements, and that given in cross-examination and re-examination. In Crown Court criminal trials, judges make a note of verbal evidence from prosecution witnesses, even though they have copies of the witness statements, because what is said in court may be different from what is in the statements. Defence witnesses' evidence in chief will be noted, but not usually evidence of police interviews, because these are taped and usually an agreed written summary or extracts of the interview is put to the jury.

Apart from the judge's notes, all High Court hearings are tape-recorded. The microphones in the High Court are not for amplification but for recording. In Crown Courts a verbatim record is made, either by tape-recording or by a stenographer. Some County Court proceedings are taped, although hearings in district judges' private rooms are often not. In magistrates' courts one of the clerk's jobs is to make a note of the evidence.

Reporting of the proceedings

The press can attend any hearing which is not private, which includes hearings in magistrates' courts, including youth courts but not family courts. They can also attend Crown Courts and County and High Court hearings, other than family proceedings. The press can report anything that is said other than in private, including the evidence of witnesses. Most reporters are not specialists, so reports of anything remotely technical are likely to be no better than partially accurate, and in any event only perceived highlights are picked out, which may give a distorted view of what the case was about and what actually happened.

A consultation exercise is being undertaken in relation to the suggestion that there would be more confidence in some of the difficult and controversial decisions of family courts if the proceedings could be reported in the press.

An important element of English law is precedent, that is, decisions in earlier cases. Decisions on new points of law need to be disseminated and so professional law reporters decide whether judgments, usually only those of the High Court, Court of Appeal or House of Lords, are worth reporting. Specialist law reports are published periodically, like magazines.

ACTIVITY 8.4

Law reports appear in the Times *on most days when the High Court is sitting. Other news-papers usually publish them weekly, and they are available on various websites (see below). They are worth reading to give you a flavour of legal decision-making, and it would be helpful to keep any cuttings which relate to decisions in cases within your particular area of interest.*

The next example contains a stark warning about attending court: however well-prepared you are, there is always a risk that something surprising, or even shocking, will occur. In such a situation, you will have to draw on all your resources to maintain your professional role, and be sure to seek support during supervision afterwards.

CASE EXAMPLE

I was sitting behind the lawyers at the start of a hearing in which the local authority was taking care proceedings on the basis of the circumstances surrounding the death of a previous child when, without warning, photographs of the post-mortem examination of the child were passed back for everyone to look at. I subsequently found it very difficult to concentrate on what was happening in court. I still do not understand why it was necessary for this to happen, and of course I now realise that my feelings were nothing as compared with how it must have affected the parents. (Social worker)

CHAPTER SUMMARY

In this chapter we have explored the order in which things happen in criminal, civil and family courts. We encourage you to make full use of your observation skills whenever you are at court, since this will enable you to develop an understanding of the different roles of those involved, and we hope it will be reassuring to you to have a reasonable idea of what is likely to happen at each stage. However, there is always the possibility that something unexpected will happen.

WEBSITES

www.lawreports.co.uk
The Incorporated Council of Law Reporting.

www.timesonline.co.uk
Law reports available free for three weeks following publication.

Chapter 9
Giving evidence

A C H I E V I N G   A   S O C I A L   W O R K   D E G R E E

This chapter addresses the communication skills defined within QAA subject benchmarks for social work, and will help you meet the following national occupational standards for social work:

Key role 5: Manage and be accountable, with supervision and support, for your own social work practice within your organisation.
- Carry out duties using accountable professional judgment and knowledge-based social work practice.
- Provide evidence for judgments and decisions.

Key role 6: Demonstrate professional competence in social work practice.
- Review and update your own knowledge of legal, policy and procedural frameworks.
- Exercise and justify professional judgments.
- Use professional assertiveness to justify decisions and uphold professional social work practice, values and ethics.

Introduction

In this chapter we look at the mechanics of giving evidence. We have already explained that, unless you are a witness of fact in criminal proceedings, your main evidence, the *evidence in chief*, is presented in a written statement. How to deal with cross-examination on your evidence is considered in the next chapter.

Social workers' status as witnesses

The case of *F* v. *Suffolk County Council* (1981) 2 FLR 208 established that qualified social workers can be regarded by courts as experts in childcare issues. However, they do not have the status of experts in relation to the diagnosis of sexual abuse (*Re N* (1996) 2 FLR 2), nor in relation to whether children's evidence can be accepted.

You may find it surprising, in view of the emphasis on collaborative and inter-disciplinary working, that in court you are not giving evidence as a member of a team, but as an individual. As an employee, you obviously have to follow the instructions of your managers; if, for example, it is decided in a case conference to recommend the initiation of care proceedings and you are instructed to take this forward, then you must do this. However, once in court, your primary duty is to the court, which requires you to give evidence of your personal knowledge and opinions, not those of anyone else. You do not have to support the line of the party on whose behalf you are giving evidence if, on professional grounds, you do not. This can be difficult, particularly if you are relatively inexperienced, but it is important. If the court wishes to hear from your team or service manager, or anyone else, then they can be called as a witness, and indeed should be if their views and decisions are important to the case.

CASE EXAMPLE

In a case where one of the matters at issue was the likelihood or otherwise of a family being allocated council housing and where the social worker had included in her witness statement details of the housing department's position as set out in correspondence, the court ordered the housing manager to give evidence. Perhaps not surprisingly, the manager presented to the court a more optimistic view than the one given previously to the social worker.

This example shows how careful you must be when representing the views of anyone else.

Must you give evidence?

In most cases, the answer is yes. Anyone can be required to attend court if their evidence is considered relevant in care proceedings, and if you are the case social worker your evidence will be relevant. You are also not likely to be entitled to anonymity, even if you are apprehensive about possible consequences, as made clear in *Re W (Children) (Care Proceedings: Witness Anonymity)* [2002] EWCA Civ 1626 when the Court of Appeal said: *Cases in which the court will afford anonymity to a professional social work witness will be highly exceptional.*

Preparation for giving evidence in chief

If you are called as a witness, it is important to re-read your witness statement before you give evidence. In civil cases you do not have to try to remember everything because your written statement is available to you as you give your evidence. However, you do have to confirm that it is true, so you should read it carefully. If, when asked whether you have read your statement recently, you say *no*, you will probably have to sit there and read it, which may embarrass you and make the process of giving evidence more difficult. It may also mean that in your anxiety to get to the end you will not read it carefully enough. Notice typographical errors and make a note to correct them. Failure to correct errors looks unprofessional and may cast doubt on the quality of your evidence.

When to go into the witness box

Television films tend to give the impression that when it is time for you to give evidence someone in court will shout out, *Call* [your name], and this is echoed by a number of officials until the message reaches you. In practice, this is not what happens at all.

In civil or family proceedings you are normally present in court when it is time for you to give evidence. Occasionally witnesses are asked to wait outside the courtroom, but it is unusual. In criminal proceedings it is different, because it is thought important that witnesses do not hear other witnesses' evidence until they have completed their own. Therefore, if you are a witness of fact in a criminal trial, someone will tell you where to wait and when you are required.

What to do while waiting to go into the witness box

Court proceedings take much longer than you might imagine. Any case other than the most straightforward will last hours and possibly days, and so if you are a witness in a criminal trial, or supporting someone who is, you should bring plenty to read while you are waiting. Witnesses of fact in criminal trials should not have any contact with the defendant or any of the lawyers acting for anyone other than the person on whose behalf they are giving evidence.

How to go into the witness box

This might seem to be a strange thing to comment on, but some judges do not like it if your route to the witness box takes you between the lawyers and the judge. Choose a route which takes you from wherever you are sitting or entering the court, round the back of the rows of lawyers, to the witness box. Move calmly, and try not to rush or drop anything which you are taking with you.

What to take with you into the witness box

There are no cloakrooms at courts, so if you are wearing a coat or carrying a briefcase, you will have to bring them with you into the courtroom. You should not, however, take them into the witness box; they can be left on, or under, a seat in the part of the court used by the public. If you are the main representative of the local authority in the case, you may be asked to sit next to the solicitor acting for the authority, so that the barrister who sits in front can talk to you during the hearing, a process called *taking instructions*. If you are sitting next to the solicitor, you can leave your coat and briefcase there. There is no reason why you should not take your handbag with you, but space in the witness box is limited and so it is best to put it on the floor beside it. Remember to take anything which you may need as an aid to giving evidence, such as your glasses.

Usually a set of the bundles of documents in the case is placed in the witness box before you come to give evidence. These should include a copy of your witness statement and also copies of any documents to which you may be asked to refer. You need not, therefore, take with you your witness statement or the case file unless specifically asked to do so. You should, however, know where your file is in court, in case you need to refer to it. You should never take into the witness box any notes which you may have made about the case for your own use, like comments on the witness statements of others. If you do, you will probably find your private thoughts being shared with everyone else present.

The oath

When you arrive in the witness box you should stay standing. Before starting to give evidence, all witnesses must either take an oath or affirm. It is your choice and you have a right to affirm if you wish. If you take the oath, you should be asked on which holy book you wish to take it.

That's the theory.

In practice you will probably find the court usher asking, *What religion are you?* and assuming that you will swear on the holy book of that religion, if there is a copy in court. Courts often do not have even the holy books of the principal religions represented in this country today. If the usher cannot immediately find the book on which you wish to swear, it may be suggested that you swear on the New Testament. However, if there is a copy in the building of the relevant holy book, reasonable efforts should be made to obtain it for you. If it is not available, you can be required to affirm. The affirmation of a witness is: *I do solemnly, sincerely and truly declare and affirm that the evidence I shall give shall be the truth, the whole truth and nothing but the truth*.

If your religion requires any preliminaries to be completed before an oath can be taken, such as washing, you should have an opportunity to carry them out. Holy books of religions which prohibit the handling of scripture other than by the ritually pure are usually kept in a cloth cover, and if you wish to swear on such a book, it should be handed to you in its cover. You should remove it from the cover, and replace it after the oath has been taken.

The oath taken by a witness who is a Christian is: *I swear by Almighty God that the evidence I shall give shall be the truth, the whole truth and nothing but the truth*. Christians swear on the New Testament. If taken by a member of another religion, the words *Almighty God* are replaced with the name of the appropriate designation of God, such as *Allah*, or, if it is the custom to swear by the book itself, the name of the book, as in *I swear by the Bhagavad Gita*.

The taking of the oath or the making of an affirmation is important to the person concerned as it is a solemn promise to tell the truth, and it is also an important part of the judicial process. An affirmation has the same force and effect as an oath, and if you tell lies under oath or having affirmed, you can be prosecuted for perjury. There should be silence while the oath is being taken or an affirmation made. The book on which the oath is taken should be held in a raised hand. This does not have to be the right hand, although you would not think so from the number of times the person administering the oath says *take the book in your right hand*.

What happens if you swear on the wrong book, or stumble over the words? The important thing is that the person swearing the oath considers it to be binding, even if the wrong words or book are used. In *R* v. *Kemble* (1990) 91 Cr. App. R. 178, a Muslim witness swore on the New Testament. He said that he considered an oath sworn on any holy book was binding on his conscience, and it was held that his oath was valid. You don't get off the hook if you swear on a holy book and do not believe in the religion whose holy book it is – the oath is still valid.

Sit or stand?

Witnesses in civil trials or family hearings are usually allowed to sit. A good rule of thumb is that if a chair is provided, it is there to be used. However, some judges prefer witnesses to ask if they may sit before doing so. Just because there is a chair, does not mean that you have to use it. It is difficult to feel relaxed in a chair without arms, or when the height of the witness box interferes with the view of the courtroom. You may be more comfortable standing so that, for example, you can reach all of the witness bundles. You may also feel more in control, as the lawyer who cross-examines you will also be standing. If you stand, your body language may be more obvious to others in the court, but as we discuss below, this is likely to be of more concern to you than anyone else. If you are really nervous and feel shaky, hold on to the edge of the witness box or the chair. In criminal trials witnesses normally stand while giving evidence and often there is no chair in the witness box. If you need a chair, ask for one, but you may be asked to explain why you want to sit. Surprisingly, you may find that *I have been standing giving evidence for four hours and I am tired* is not usually considered sufficient.

Volume and speed

It is important to be prepared for how loudly you need to speak when giving evidence and at what speed. As we have said, if there are microphones in court, they are not for amplification but to record the proceedings. It is most important that your evidence is heard by the magistrates or judge, the jury if there is one and the lawyers who are doing the questioning. If any of these cannot hear you, you will be asked to speak up, which can be off-putting if you are nervous, and if it happens several times there is a risk that the judge will become irritated. Before you give evidence, try and assess other speakers in the court, so that you get an idea of how loudly you will need to speak, but don't shout. You will be fascinated to know that judges have hearing tests when they are appointed and do not need to be harangued as if they were in a public meeting.

ACTIVITY **9.1**

- *Observe people presenting their views, or answering questions, in a variety of settings (television discussion programme, chat show, church service, lecture, party political broadcast).*

- *Note what seems to support effective communication in terms of volume and speed, and what creates barriers between the speaker and listener.*

- *What changes do you think you might need to make in relation to your own presentation skills?*

This activity shows that you can improve your presentation skills by careful observation in the course of everyday activities.

You may be advised by a lawyer to *follow his Lordship's pen*. This is supposed to encourage you to give your evidence at dictation speed, so that the judge can write it all down. However, while judges do make a note of the evidence, they do not need to write down every single word. A judge who is finding it difficult to keep up will certainly say so. Don't be distracted from concentrating on the questions you are being asked and the answers you want to give by trying to look in a direction in which you would not otherwise be looking. Watching the speed at which a judge writes is about as interesting as watching grass grow. Usually, when lawyers tell you to *follow his Lordship's pen*, they are really telling the judge to make a careful note of the evidence. Some lawyers manage, perhaps inadvertently, to distract witnesses and make their task even more difficult by saying something like, *I shall be asking you the questions, but direct your answers to his Lordship/the magistrates*. If you complied with this instruction you would be twisting and turning every time you were asked a question. What is important is that your answers are heard by everyone. It is not easy to make a note of what is being said while looking at a witness, so the judge is likely to be concentrating on taking notes, rather than looking at you.

Verbal additions to your witness statement

When you have taken the oath or affirmed you have promised to tell *the whole truth*. Does anyone really want to hear it? The answer is probably no. However, you may wish to add something to your witness statement, perhaps because of a further thought, or as a comment on another witness statement, because you have been reminded of something or because something significant has happened since you wrote it. If you do want to add anything, you should tell the lawyer acting for the party on whose behalf you have been called to give evidence. They can then advise whether you should mention it and, if so, give you an opportunity at the start of your evidence. However, if the lawyer does not think that the matter is worth mentioning but you do, or the lawyer forgets to give you the opportunity, you should mention it before you confirm the accuracy of your witness statement if it affects something in that statement, or before your cross-examination begins if it is something new. After all, the evidence is yours, not the lawyer's, and no one should try to prevent you telling the story from your point of view as you remember it.

We deal with points which occur to you while you are being cross-examined in the next chapter.

Body language

Body language is generally of more interest to social workers than it is to lawyers and this is considered further in Chapter 11, when we explain how judges make decisions. The judge is likely to be too busy making notes to pay much attention to how you sit or whether you fiddle with your glasses, and lawyers are not trained to interpret body language as are social workers. If you do have some mannerisms which suggest that you are feeling uncomfortable or nervous, judges are unlikely to attach much significance to them, even if they notice them. For judges and lawyers, courts are part of their work environment, but many witnesses will never achieve that level of familiarity with them. Most courts understand that and take account of it and so, if you show that you are nervous, no one will be surprised. What your body language may convey to others in court is also not likely to be very significant. Anyone else is really just a spectator, and they may well be sympathetic to you in what they recognise as an ordeal. It is, however, sensible to be aware of the possibility of any negative feelings you may have being leaked through non-verbal means (see the example in Chapter 10).

Relevance

It is not for you to decide whether any of the questions which you are asked is relevant. If any of the lawyers, or the judge, think that a question has been asked, the answer to which would be irrelevant, they will say so. Broadly, what is relevant is factual evidence, your analysis and opinions, evidence of your reliability as a witness, and evidence of your qualifications to express the opinions which you have, which can include evidence as to the quality of your memory, hearing, eyesight or propensity to be truthful and honest.

Interruptions in the evidence

Unless your evidence is very short, it will probably be interrupted by an adjournment for lunch or at the end of the day. Even in civil or family cases, if there is an adjournment during your evidence you should not discuss it, or any issues in the case, with anyone. Sometimes witnesses are reminded of this rule and sometimes they are not. The reason for it is that your evidence should be your own, uninfluenced by anything that anyone else may say to you. If you were to talk to someone about your evidence, they might say *Why did you not mention so and so?* or *Why did you have to say that?* which could affect how you give the rest of your evidence. Barristers are prohibited by their professional rules from having contact about the case with witnesses until their evidence has finished without the consent of the lawyers for the other parties or the court and you should observe the same rule. You can certainly say *Good morning*, or talk about anything other than the case, but it avoids misunderstanding if you do not speak to them at all, unless loudly enough for the other parties to hear what you are saying. However, this can make you feel very isolated and unsupported if you are giving lengthy evidence in a complex case.

Changes and additions during the course of giving evidence

Inevitably you will reflect on your evidence during adjournments, which may result in you remembering something you should have said, or perhaps being concerned that something you did say has been misunderstood, or even incorrectly presented. If this happens, you should raise it when you return to the witness box. However, a note of caution: too dramatic a change in your evidence after a break may give the impression that you have been nobbled by someone during the adjournment.

Relations with other parties

Although litigation is an adversarial process, it does not have to be conducted in a hostile way, and a lot depends on the nature of the case and the personalities of those involved. There is no rule which prevents barristers from exchanging pleasantries with another party's witnesses, but they should not discuss details of the case or the evidence. Barristers and solicitors should be courteous in all their professional dealings, but inevitably you will warm to some more than others. However, stereotypical assumptions about the legal profession will prove to be a significant barrier to effective working relationships (see Activity 3.1 in Chapter 3).

> *It is really difficult knowing what to say to the family when you arrive at court. You don't know whether to say 'hello', knowing you are likely to be ignored or may appear patronising, or collude with the adversarial atmosphere by saying nothing.* (Child protection social worker)

In family cases involving children, confrontation should be avoided as far as possible, and so, although it may be difficult because of the nature of the issues at stake, everyone should try to achieve an atmosphere which is as least tense as possible. If you are involved in a case in which an order is sought against your client, you are probably going to have to continue to work with that client (unlike the lawyers), so there is no point doing anything other than trying to maintain professional relationships during the proceedings. However, it would not be surprising if they wanted to have as little as possible to do with you. Unless you have personal experience of what they are facing, you cannot begin to understand what they are feeling, and it would be patronising to suggest that you do. It can be very difficult if you become the focus of hostility when you are only doing your job, but in distressing circumstances, it is not uncommon to look for someone to bear the brunt of strong feelings and you should always be sensitive towards those for whom a great deal may be at stake.

ACTIVITY 9.2

A study of judicial decision-making and the management of care proceedings (Iwaniec et al., 2004) *found that once experts' reports were initiated, courts were reluctant to accept social workers as both 'prosecutors' and objective witnesses. What actions on the part of the social worker would help address this?*

This activity encourages you to think creatively about the dilemmas presented by your sometimes conflicting roles at court. It requires you to analyse your professional responsibilities and, drawing on what we have said about fairness and impartiality, consider how you can encourage lawyers, judges and service users to have confidence in your objectivity.

After cross-examination

After cross-examination, the lawyer on whose behalf the witness was called has the opportunity to re-examine them. Don't try to leave the witness box as soon as cross-examination is over, although it is tempting. However, re-examination does not happen in every case. Whether or not there is re-examination, it is conventional for the lawyer who has called a witness to ask if there is anything the judge wishes to ask. Judges differ as to how they obtain information from witnesses. Some leave it all to the lawyers and ask few, if any, questions. This does not mean that the judge has not been interested in your evidence, but rather that everything necessary had been covered. Some judges ask questions during the cross-examination or re-examination as matters occur to them, and others save up everything to the end. If a judge asks questions at the end of the evidence, the lawyers are usually given the opportunity to ask any further questions which arise out of the questions and the witness's responses.

C H A P T E R S U M M A R Y

This chapter has explored some of the practicalities and rules of giving evidence, and also the preparation and skills required to reduce the tensions which may arise in the course of working with others during the process.

Bond, C., Solon, M. and Harper, P. (1999) *The Expert Witness in Court: A Practical Guide*, 2nd edn. Crayford: Shaw.
This text offers advice on giving evidence.

www.jsboard.co.uk
The website of the Judicial Studies Board has information about taking oaths in court.

Chapter 10
Cross-examination

> **A C H I E V I N G   A   S O C I A L   W O R K   D E G R E E**
>
> This chapter addresses the problem-solving and communication skills defined within QAA subject benchmarks for social work, and will help you meet the following national occupational standards for social work:
>
> *Key role 5: Manage and be accountable, with supervision and support, for your own social work practice within your organisation.*
> * Carry out duties using accountable professional judgment and knowledge-based social work practice.
> * Provide evidence for judgments and decisions.
>
> *Key role 6: Demonstrate professional competence in social work practice.*
> * Exercise and justify professional judgments.
> * Use professional assertiveness to justify decisions and uphold professional social work practice, values and ethics.

Introduction

Cross-examination takes place in both criminal and civil proceedings and is the part of the trial process which is often most daunting to witnesses. Even the term *cross-examination* may be intimidating, suggesting something hostile in the course of which the questioner becomes *cross*. This is misleading, since the process need not be, and usually is not, hostile, particularly in family proceedings. However, it is never likely to be particularly pleasant, not least because the anticipation of an ordeal usually contributes as much, if not more, stress than the experience itself.

It is easy for someone who is not used to giving evidence to imagine that all sorts of terrors lie in wait once they enter the witness box to be cross-examined.

* Will the judge be sympathetic or intimidating?

* Will the advocates set out to make me look stupid?

* Will they try to bully me, or trick me into saying things that I do not mean?

* What happens if I forget something important, or get confused?

You may also have been worried by hearing anecdotal evidence of other people's experiences in the witness box.

These fears, which are entirely natural, may also stem from dramatic representations of cross-examination on television, or in films, in which the starring lawyer triumphantly demolishes the evidence of the key witness or, at the eleventh hour, produces material, as if out of a hat, which undermines the whole prosecution (or defence) case. These dramatic representations cannot give a realistic idea of the court process. Plays or films usually last less than three hours, which is little more than a morning in court. Any family court hearing is likely to last at least one court day – five hours – and may well be spread over several days. So, cross-examination is not usually a fast and furious encounter over ten or fifteen minutes, but can last an hour or more, or possibly even days.

For social workers facing cross-examination on their evidence, preparation and understanding the way in which advocates approach the task will help make the experience more manageable. As the aim of cross-examination is to expose any flaws in the evidence, it follows that evidence which has been properly prepared and presented by people who are familiar with their material, confident in their role, clear about the rationale for any opinions expressed and understand what is likely to happen has the best chance of standing up to scrutiny. We have explored the importance of presentation and use of language and, as much as anything else, this will support you when facing cross-examination. However, it is also useful to understand its purpose and how lawyers approach the task.

The purpose of cross-examination

Contrary to the impression often created by films and television, the purpose of cross-examination is not entertainment of the public through the discomfort of the witness, orchestrated by a seasoned and experienced verbal assassin, the barrister, in a sort of modern-day gladiatorial combat. The only proper purpose of cross-examination is to give all parties in a case the opportunity, usually through their advocate, to challenge the evidence of other parties. In this way, evidence can be tested for accuracy, consistency and authenticity. If a witness's evidence is accepted, there is no need for cross-examination, because there is nothing about which questions need to be asked. As there is only a need to cross-examine witnesses on contested evidence, the scope of cross-examination may be quite narrow. On the other hand, if a party wishes to challenge the way in which a local authority has managed the whole of a client's case, it may be necessary and appropriate for their advocate to ask the social worker numerous and detailed questions about what decisions were made, what actions were taken or not taken, and why.

What are witnesses likely to be asked about in cross-examination?

As we have seen, evidence is likely to come in either or both of two categories: fact and opinion.

Evidence of fact is evidence of what a witness has perceived by use of one of their senses – that is, what they have seen, heard, touched, smelled or tasted.

Possible reasons for challenging evidence of fact include the following:

- *Perception* It may be suggested that a witness's perception at the time of the event in question is wrong; for example, while the witness was observing a period of contact between a parent and child, something relevant happened which the witness did not notice, or which they did notice, but misinterpreted.

- *Memory* Evidence often relates to events which occurred months, or even years, previously and it could be suggested that a witness's memory has faded, so that relevant matters have been partially or completely forgotten. This is why accurate and comprehensive record-keeping is so important.

- *Bias or prejudice* Although not very likely in relation to professional witnesses, a cross-examining advocate could suggest that a witness is biased or prejudiced against their client for some reason. Social workers are fortunate in that they normally have the benefit of professional supervision, which should ensure that facts are accurate and decisions are supported by a clear rationale. However, it is vitally important to maintain objectivity, which may on occasions mean disclosing information which does not support the case of the party for whom you have been called to give evidence.

- *Lying* It is possible that a witness could be accused in cross-examination of deliberately giving an inaccurate account – telling lies. It is not expected that a social worker, or any professional witness, will ever tell lies on oath, and it is very unlikely that an advocate would consider it appropriate to suggest such a thing. Yet it is when that suggestion is being made that cross-examination is most likely to become confrontational, distressing to the witness and most like how it is represented on television and in films. As we have seen, lawyers act under a set of professional rules and it is professional misconduct for a barrister to *make statements or ask questions which are merely scandalous or intended or calculated only to vilify, insult or annoy either a witness or some other person*. It follows that advocates should not make suggestions of lying or other discreditable conduct on the part of professional witnesses, unless it is necessary to their client's case to do so and there are solid grounds to support them. In other words, normally you need have no fear of hurtful or distressing questions being put which cast doubt upon your personal integrity.

Evidence of opinion is evidence of what the witness thinks about something. Usually, evidence of opinion may not be given in court. However, as we have seen, there is an exception in relation to matters requiring expert knowledge. Expert knowledge is acquired by training or experience, or a combination of both. If another party calls an expert witness who expresses a different opinion from the one you have formed, you will inevitably be cross-examined about it. On professional matters, different people can legitimately hold different views, which in itself is not a reason for criticism. However, in contested legal proceedings, where differences in professional opinion are important, one of the judge's tasks is to decide which opinion to accept. Judges are not equipped by academic or professional training to form views on professional social work issues, and so they must listen to those who express competing views and decide which to accept. They can, in fact, accept neither and take a middle course, but any decision must be based on relevant grounds of distinction between the different opinions.

Possible reasons for challenging evidence of opinion include the following:

- *Level of expertise* Structural engineers are qualified and likely to be experienced in the design of the structure of buildings. They are therefore, in law, experts, but only in relation to the design of the structure of buildings. They are not experts in matters of childcare, and no one would dream of suggesting that they were. To be qualified to give opinion evidence means being able to offer evidence which goes beyond a level of understanding which might be found in a person of reasonable intelligence. However, what is often found in family proceedings is overlapping between different professionals. There may be medical, psychiatric or psychological evidence, in addition to more than one source of social work evidence. It could be that a social worker's view about the best way to promote the future development of a child is different from that of the child psychologist called on behalf of the parents. The children's guardian may not fully support the local authority's plan. In such cases, the court has to decide which witness is best qualified to express an opinion on the matter in dispute. It cannot be said that the evidence of a psychologist or children's guardian should always be preferred to that of a social worker or vice versa, since everything depends on the issues in the case. However, where there is disputed evidence, cross-examination of the social worker will have as one of its objectives to demonstrate to the court that the social worker is not as well equipped as the other professionals to express an opinion. This sort of cross-examination should not be a cause of distress or upset. It is not a criticism of someone with one set of professional qualifications that they do not possess a different set of professional qualifications. This is so, even if the court ultimately decides that one person is better qualified to express a view than another.

  Each of us claims some knowledge of the law relating to social work, and where the issue was essentially legal, such as the interpretation of an Act of Parliament, you may prefer the opinion of the legally qualified author. On the other hand, if the issue was essentially one of social work practice, you would be likely to consider the opinion of the qualified social worker as more valuable. So it is with differing opinion evidence from professionals from different disciplines. However, we acknowledge that it can be frustrating when other expert witnesses appear to overstep what you consider are professional boundaries when expressing their opinions. In such cases it is important to avoid being defensive, and to remain focused on the rationale for the opinions you have formed.

- *Level of experience* We do not want to overemphasise the significance of this, but if two social workers who express different opinions are, on the one hand, someone newly qualified and inexperienced and, on the other, a highly qualified person with many years' practice experience, the court may prefer the evidence of the latter. In such a case, the cross-examination of the newly qualified social worker might have as one of its aims to demonstrate that they lacked sufficient experience. This should not be taken as personal criticism, since no one can produce experience which they do not have.

- *Range of experience* Although social work qualifying training is generic, most social work practice and post-qualifying training is specialist, so that a social worker will usually only be working with one specific client group at any one time. This means that a social worker with many years of experience of mental health work, who has recently moved into a childcare team, may have it suggested in cross-examination that their limited experience of childcare casts doubt on the validity of their opinions in a family case. Again, this should not be taken as a personal criticism, and we suggest that if you are a qualified social worker, you should feel confident in the value of your generic training, supported by GSCC registration requirements in relation to continuing professional development.

- *Rationale* Notwithstanding what we have said about qualifications and experience, it is far from inevitable that the court will prefer the evidence of the more experienced practitioner if the newly qualified social worker has good grounds for their opinion, which are clearly expressed. It is therefore important that, when preparing for cross-examination, you should have a good grasp of the rationale behind any opinions you have offered, which should incorporate the four *Rs* described in Chapter 7.

How advocates approach cross-examination

Advocacy, which includes conducting cross-examination, is part of legal training, and a textbook published by the College of Law (Elkington et al., 2004, p129) introduces law students to the skills of cross-examination in this way:

> In order to conduct cross-examination effectively, it is necessary to develop a 'theory' of the client's case. This theory should be a plausible version of the events, consistent with the available evidence and the client's instructions which, if accepted, will result in the court finding in the client's favour.

However, some lawyers believe that skills in cross-examination cannot be taught, but depend more on how particular advocates approach the task and the level of their experience. Some eminent barristers have not been very effective cross-examiners and others do not particularly enjoy the task. However, for many, cross-examination represents the point at which their legal knowledge and advocacy skills come together in an exercise which is potentially challenging, exciting or even exhilarating. We recall the long-awaited opportunity to cross-examine a particularly notorious witness in a long-running case as one of the highlights of a legal career.

An effective cross-examiner is one who succeeds in obtaining from another party's witness evidence which assists their client's case, which means obtaining answers which the witness accepts are accurate, or at least more accurate than their previous evidence. After cross-examination, the advocate for the party calling a witness can ask further questions to clarify the answers given in cross-examination. This stage of the evidence is called re-examination, and is limited to any new issues which have arisen out of cross-examination, rather than going over evidence which has already been given. If a witness has been persuaded by the style of cross-examination to say something which they did not mean, then this is likely to become apparent in re-examination, when there is an opportunity to correct the previous answer. The effective cross-examiner is therefore looking to achieve an impact which cannot be reversed in re-examination, which depends on presenting the witness with material which changes their perception of the fact or opinion about which they are being asked. Clearly, nervousness or confusion can influence a witness's answers, which is why we hope that understanding of the process will make this less likely to occur.

Effective cross-examination depends upon thorough preparation and good command of the material available. It is worth remembering that if an advocate puts a question during cross-examination which suggests that there is a relevant document which supports the point of the question, this is probably true, because it will have been found during the preparation of the case. It would be very unwise for a cross-examiner to suggest to a witness a version of events which could not be supported by reference to evidence. It used to be said that student barristers were told during training: *Never ask a question to which you do not know the answer*. That may be apocryphal, but it does illustrate that in order to try to persuade a witness to agree to or change their mind about something, the cross-examiner needs to be in command of all the relevant facts and able to produce supporting material.

Unlike in examination-in-chief, advocates can ask leading questions during cross-examination, although they should not make statements without giving the witness the opportunity to comment on them. The most basic style of cross-examination, and that most familiar from films and television, is somewhat as follows:

Cross-examiner: I put it to you that your evidence is a pack of lies.

Witness: No, it isn't.

Cross-examiner: Yes, it is.

Witness: No, it isn't.

This is more reminiscent of a pantomime than the courtroom. Only once in a professional career did one of us suggest to a witness that his participation in a particular enterprise was simply a means of stealing money and, surprisingly, receive the answer *yes*. Barring the odd exception, cross-examination by putting an accusation to a witness, and repeating it if they do not agree, is a waste of time. Effective cross-examination depends upon producing material which persuades witnesses to alter their evidence and, if such material exists, in the majority of cases it is in documentary form.

Styles of cross-examination

Having said that cross-examination is a rather inexact science, there are nevertheless discernible styles which can be observed, sometimes in combination.

- *Organised and predictable* Some quite eminent and successful lawyers prepare thoroughly for cross-examination, to the extent of writing out a list of questions in advance. Cross-examination then takes the form of going through the questions. This is not especially difficult to handle, because the questions are usually posed in the order in which they have been written, without regard to the answers obtained in the meantime.

- *Intellectually challenging* Cross-examiners who maintain the intellectual flexibility to pursue answers which seem relevant to their client's case will have an outline plan which they can adjust as required. Many advocates are able to think on their feet, adapting their questions according to the answers given. They may also try to unsettle the witness, by taking events out of chronological order. This kind of cross-examination can be very tiring.

- *Intimidating* Occasionally advocates set out to dominate and intimidate witnesses with a loud voice and superior manner. This may have some theatrical appeal, but is usually less effective than a quieter, more respectful style. If a witness's answers in cross-examination have been obtained by an advocate who has been sympathetic, they may well appear to the court to be more persuasive. This is particularly true in family proceedings, where advocates are expected to avoid an adversarial approach and the primary focus is the welfare of the child, rather than who wins or loses.

- *Chaotic* While not exactly a style of cross-examination, you may be surprised to find that some advocates appear incapable of asking a simple question, sometimes posing several questions at once, while expecting one *yes* or *no* answer. This is not usually a deliberate ploy to confuse the witness, but rather evidence of the limitations of the advocate as a cross-examiner.

- *Unprepared* A variation on the chaotic is the cross-examiner who is simply not on top of the material and who poses questions based on a misunderstanding or lack of knowledge of the facts or issues. Unfortunately, this seems to be becoming more common as restrictions on public funding of legal costs influence the time which advocates have for, or are prepared to devote to, preparing for cross-examination. While many advocates are competent at cross-examination, and are conscientious in preparing for it, you should not assume that all lawyers are skilled cross-examiners.

- *Softening-up* Some advocates adopt a technique which involves asking a series of fairly innocuous, simple and uncontroversial questions before moving on to a more assertive line of questioning. The hope is that the witness will relax and continue to agree when more contentious matters are put to them.

- *Unpleasant* There are, regrettably, a very few advocates whose style of cross-examination is bullying, sarcastic and intended to cause distress and discomfort to witnesses while remaining, by a whisker, within their rules of professional conduct. Fortunately, they are not often encountered, particularly in family proceedings, but if you do experience it, be assured that it is not a legitimate style of cross-examination, but rather a reflection of the personality, and possibly professional inadequacy, of the advocate. Such behaviour will not pass the judge unnoticed and may well be the subject of judicial censure.

Types of question

In social work interviews, the distinction is usually made between open and closed questions, and these are also used to different effect in cross-examination. For example, a closed question may be used to press for an admission of some sort when a witness would prefer to add explanatory material, or qualify their answer. You also need to be able to recognise the three broad categories of cross-examination question – probing, insinuating and confrontational – each of which may trigger a different instinctive response. As an expert witness, you are most likely to encounter the first type, which are easiest to deal with if you follow the advice below about listening carefully to the question, keeping your answer brief and focused, and avoiding jargon and clichés. Insinuating and confrontational questions are more difficult, since your first reaction may be defensiveness.

Although in principle you are not allowed to ask questions yourself, it may be worth asking what the actual question is in these circumstances. The next example, in which the advocate seems to be suggesting that because it was not an average case, it should not have received a routine response, shows that it is sometimes possible to deflect an insinuation, gain some extra thinking time and reduce it to something more manageable.

CASE EXAMPLE

Victoria Climbié Inquiry, 4 October 2001

Q: *But this case was not quite the ordinary case that you were dealing with, simply housing issues, because you have noted some of your other concerns about the case – the fact that she has children in France and intends to return.*

A: *Was that a question?*

Q: *Yes.*

A: *What was the question?*

Q: *Well, it seems looking at it that there are issues that go beyond the simple case of housing ... it was not quite the average case you were dealing with.*

A: *Well, it was not an average case because she did come from France and part of her family was in France.*

Confrontational questions sometimes follow probing questions, if the cross-examiner considers it worth pressing for particular answers. This is another reason why focused responses are important. Vagueness or elusiveness in an answer may encourage the advocate to become more confrontational in an effort to extract some kind of admission.

How to handle cross-examination

The best social workers answer the question fairly and honourably, concede a little if necessary but, as is their duty, stick to their guns. For example: Yes, I agree that David is much better at controlling his temper and the school is pleased. However, I think we still have a long way to go. The parents love him very much and he loves them, but I still don't think that they can give him the care he needs. (Family court judge)

While too much preparation can be counterproductive, in that it may fuel anxiety and deflect you from the main issues in the case, it is worth identifying strategies which may support you in the witness box.

- **Don't take it personally** You should always try to approach cross-examination in a professional manner, which, as you will know from your practice, requires a certain amount of resilience, assertiveness and detachment. In asking questions, advocates are performing their professional duty to their client, and this may mean that they are asked to put something to you which you regard as outrageous (for example, that you have been racist in your dealings with someone). If this happens, try not to take personally any suggestions made, even if you feel that they reflect on your professional competence. Your professional competence is not in any event, as already explained, something to feel sensitive about, even if another party's expert may appear to be better qualified, have more experience, or simply hold another view. It is important to appear calm and objective, both verbally and non-verbally. Even though you may feel indignant, or even insulted, nothing is gained by showing this, and it may harm your credibility as a professional witness if you reveal your personal feelings.

CASE EXAMPLE

I remember fighting a losing battle with the tendency to stand with my hands on my hips during a very long drawn-out cross-examination, thus unfortunately suggesting an attitude which was more confrontational than conciliatory. This would have been less of a problem had I been sitting down. (Social worker)

- *Are you going to play the game?* To the skilled advocate, cross-examination is essentially an intellectual game for two players, one of whom is you. Most importantly from your point of view, the advocate cannot play without you, and this critical fact gives you more control over the process than you may think. For example, if you are unable, or do not wish, to give the answer which the advocate hopes for, no one can force you.

- *Establish the ground rules* If, as sometimes happens, a question is confusing, you are entitled to say that you do not understand it and ask for it to be clarified. If you think that a document may help you answer, you are entitled to ask to be shown it. You are not normally entitled to ask questions of the person questioning you, unless it is for clarification. However, the advocate cannot fix the ground rules as to how you answer the questions. Sometimes an advocate will try to insist that a witness answers a question with *yes* or *no*, when neither would be a sufficient answer. Just say that the question cannot be answered with a simple *yes* or *no*, and give the answer that you want to give. The court is interested in knowing what your evidence is, not what the advocate wishes it to be.

- *Expect the unexpected* You cannot assume that you will be asked about events in chronological order. This is likely to be the order in which they are dealt with in your witness statement, but as we have seen, one approach to cross-examination is to take events out of chronological order so as to unsettle the witness and perhaps persuade them to change their view about something. Another approach is to ask essentially the same question in a different form, hoping to demonstrate inconsistency if the answers are different. These possibilities make it all the more important to listen carefully to the questions and to give considered answers. If, as a result of the style of questioning, you think that your views have not been accurately conveyed, you are entitled to say that you wish to reconsider your answers, and then state what you think the correct position is.

- *Control the pace* It is possible to gain thinking time by carefully considering each question, taking time to formulate your answer and asking for clarification of any questions which you do not fully understand. The judge is likely to intervene if questions are fired so fast as to give a witness insufficient time to answer, but if you want time to consider your answer to a question, you should ask for it. Taking time in this way will also help redress any perceived power imbalance between you and the advocate.

- **Expect to be fairly treated** One of the judge's responsibilities is to ensure that witnesses are treated fairly. The example below illustrates the fact that advocates are sometimes tempted to make comments, in addition to asking questions, during cross-examination. This should not happen unless the witness is invited to respond, and although the judge or your own advocate should be alert to any improper comments made, unfortunately they do not always achieve the necessary level of alertness. While you should not be over-sensitive, if you feel that the advocate is being offensive or unfair, you can appeal to the judge, who will decide whether it is necessary to intervene. However, an advocate may feel that it is worth risking the censure of the judge in order to attach a potentially negative connotation to a particular witness.

CASE EXAMPLE

During cross-examination, I was asked to explain the description manipulative *which I had very unwisely included in a case record some time previously (when I was, of course, very inexperienced!). The cross-examining advocate said,* It seems to me that social workers apply this description to anyone who dares to disagree with them, *at which point the judge intervened, saying to the advocate,* Miss S, that is an offensive remark and you will withdraw it. *However, the advocate was doubtless satisfied by the fact that the comment had been heard. Needless to say, I have never used the word* manipulative *since.* (Social worker)

- **Don't try to second guess** It is usually a mistake to anticipate where the line of questioning is going. If you do, you may be tempted to prepare what you consider to be the *correct* answer, rather than give the answer that you actually believe to be the truth. You may also come across to the court as someone who is not being completely open and transparent.

- **Watch out for the wolf in sheep's clothing** Beware of agreeing too readily with apparently innocuous propositions, especially if they do not relate to you personally. As we have seen, sometimes advocates will try to soften up witnesses with apparently straightforward and uncontroversial questions before pressing much more strongly for contentious admissions.

- **Keep it short** It is usually best to give as brief an answer as possible. This is most helpful to the judge, who has to concentrate on the central issues in the case and make a note of the oral evidence, and is also likely to be beneficial to you. Long or unfocused answers provide the opportunity for points to be made which might not otherwise have been obvious to the cross-examiner. In a case about a harbour in which one of us was once involved, a witness described himself as a port expert. At the start of his cross-examination he was routinely asked, *You describe yourself as a port expert?* Instead of simply agreeing, he delivered a long account of why he had so described himself, which revealed that his expertise was limited to the operation of one particular port and so he was not entitled to be regarded as an expert in ports generally.

- *Focus, focus, focus* You should confine your answer to the scope of the question posed, and not introduce new material unless absolutely necessary, otherwise there is a risk that you will alert the cross-examiner to a line of questioning not previously considered relevant. The next example, also from the Climbié Inquiry, shows a cross-examiner being offered an unexpected admission by a witness who had not carefully considered the question posed.

CASE EXAMPLE

Victoria Climbié Inquiry, 2 October 2001

Q: *Here we are at the beginning of June and you were still being asked to do an assessment. Did that surprise you, or is that normal?*

A: *I think at the time it was difficult. We usually assessed people via housing needs, rather than being child focused.*

Q: *You assessed people generally on housing needs, rather than being child focused?*

A: *Yes, at the time.*

- *Admit mistakes* It is very unlikely that everything you do in practice will stand up to detailed scrutiny, especially with the benefit of hindsight. If it is suggested that something should have been done differently, be as honest as you can and admit any shortfall in your practice. Nothing is gained by trying to defend the indefensible or making excuses for errors or omissions, and by acknowledging a mistake you are demonstrating that you are aware of the requirements of good social work practice. However, you should explore with your advocate in advance of the hearing any potential areas of difficulty which might become the focus of cross-examination, so that you are both prepared for the issue to be raised.

CASE EXAMPLE

Victoria Climbié Inquiry, 4 October 2001

Q: *Do you accept that file entry is not signed or dated?*

A: *I think my name appears at the bottom.*

Q: *Yes, sorry, but not dated?*

A: *No, it is not dated.*

Q: *Do you accept that is a shortfall?*

A: *Absolutely, yes.*

If you say something during cross-examination which you later realise is not right, or which you think may have given the wrong impression, it is important to say so. If you leave it, hoping that no one has noticed, you risk being accused of inconsistency or inaccuracy if the matter is raised later. Simply saying, *I think I might have given the wrong impression when I said ...* or *I am sorry, I made a mistake in my last reply ...* should guard against this. You should also be careful when suggesting that an external factor was to blame for any shortfall to which you admit, since you are likely to be asked what you did about it. If you did nothing, and this is the first time that you have mentioned it, then it is probably unwise to refer to it.

CASE EXAMPLE

Victoria Climbié Inquiry, 4 October 2001

Q: *Was the supervision you received from your team manager adequate?*

A: *Not at that time, no it was not.*

Q: *Did you do anything to refer your concerns about this to senior managers?*

- *You can't duck questions* When giving evidence, or being cross-examined, you cannot normally refuse to answer a question. There is an exception in most court proceedings if, by giving a truthful answer, you might lay yourself open to possible criminal charges. However, this does not apply to cases involving children (s. 98, Children Act 1989) because the welfare of children is paramount and therefore overrides any other considerations.

- *Use notes with care* As with giving evidence, you can refer to notes during cross-examination, but there is a potential pitfall. If you use notes to refresh your memory during cross-examination, lawyers for the other parties in the case will ask to look at them. Social work records are usually contained in the case file which you will have to hand over, which gives everyone the chance to look at the whole file. As it is usually unrealistic to rely on memory when being cross-examined, it is important to anticipate this by writing your records and maintaining your files in such a way as to make them fit to be shown to other people who may have different interests in the case. You will also normally be asked how long after the event you made your notes, and if the gap was more than a day or so, the accuracy of your records may be in doubt.

- *Maintain formality* Court proceedings are essentially formal and serious occasions. Some relaxation may occur during the course of a hearing, but witnesses should not take the initiative in this respect, and attempts at humour can go spectacularly wrong. One of us was once involved in a case in which an issue was whether the witness had been present when HM Queen Elizabeth had officially opened a building. He was asked in cross-examination how the Queen had arrived at the opening ceremony and replied, *On a bicycle*. Not surprisingly, his evidence on that, and on other matters, was subsequently rejected.

ACTIVITY **10.1**

Although you should never coach anyone on their evidence, it is quite easy to practise techniques for dealing with cross-examination.

Share something you have written with a colleague or friend and ask them to discover more about the content by asking you a variety of types of question (open, closed, probing, insinuating, challenging, confrontational).

If possible, have an observer to make a note of the effectiveness of different types of questions and the nature of the responses obtained. Reflect on the process with your questioner and observer, and swap roles.

C H A P T E R   S U M M A R Y

This chapter has explained the purpose of cross-examination and explored the different ways in which lawyers approach the task. We have looked at style of questioning, types of question and strategies which may support you in the witness box, illustrated by examples from practice. In offering this insider view, with advice from people who are familiar with the process, we hope that you will become more confident of your ability, not only to withstand the experience personally, but also to represent the social work profession in a formal, multi-disciplinary setting, while keeping the principles of fairness and transparency central to your practice.

FURTHER READING

Brammer, A. (2007) *Social Work Law*, 2nd edn. Harlow: Pearson Education, Chapter 4, Social worker's role in law.

Johns, R. (2007) *Using the Law in Social Work*, 3rd edn. Exeter: Learning Matters.

WEBSITE

www.victoria-climbié-inquiry.org.uk
These extensive transcripts provide a fascinating insight into the reality of cross-examination.

Chapter 11

Legal decision-making and appeals

Introduction

How judges approach decision-making seems to be an area which is particularly mysterious to non-lawyers and yet, as we show, it is really quite simple. We also consider the appeal and complaints processes.

What makes a good judge?

It used to be thought that judges could make fair and just decisions because they were endowed with superior wisdom. In common with many professions, however, judges today are more accountable and more open to criticism than they were in the past. It is not that they have lost any of the skills which they had previously. If anything, with appointment by open competition and compulsory in-service training, they are better informed and better trained, which must be a good thing. However, like social workers, judges are targets for politicians and the popular press, and being subject to public criticism is now a hazard of judicial life, especially for those involved in sentencing or judicial review cases.

It is not always appreciated that courts do not have complete freedom to do justice or what seems fair and right, and in many cases their discretion is quite limited, particularly in relation to sentencing. Sometimes judges need to interpret statute law, but ultimately they have to apply it, whatever their personal views may be. Most of the principles of common law have been laid down for many years, and as we have seen, judges below the level of the House of Lords are bound to follow previous decisions of courts higher than the one in which they sit. This is called *the doctrine of precedent*, and failure to follow the law which is binding on the judge is a ground of appeal.

In order to apply the law you need to know it, or at least where to find it, which is essentially an academic skill. As all judges have legal qualifications, they should have acquired this skill during their training, and magistrates are advised on the law by their legally qualified clerk. However, the law, like any theory, has to be applied to practice, which is a skill judges have developed during their previous legal career. A common feature of legal disputes, however, is that there is no agreement about the facts. This is not a problem for judges trying criminal cases in the Crown Court, because the jury decides on the facts and the judge tells them how to apply the law to the various permutations of facts. Any other judge, however, has to determine the contested facts to which the law has to be applied. Deciding a case is a bit like doing sudoku. You know what the rules of the game are (the law). If you apply them to which numbers are in which square (the facts of the case as the judge or magistrates find them to be), the answer should follow. However, sometimes, for example in family cases, the answer does not follow automatically. What is needed then is an assessment of what is most likely to be beneficial or, occasionally, least likely to be harmful, which is likely to be based on experience and common sense. Even in cases where applying the law to the facts produces a straightforward answer, judges and magistrates usually try to word their decisions in a way which makes them more palatable, or at least less likely to cause long-term difficulties, for the unsuccessful party.

In the open competitions which are the means by which people hoping to be judges are selected, there is a formidable array of *competences* to be demonstrated and, as social workers, you will be familiar with these means of assessment. The fundamentals of a good judge are stated to be:

- sound knowledge of the law;
- the ability to make findings of fact which are likely to be sound;
- experience of life;
- common sense.

Magistrates are expected to have the following qualities:

- intelligence;
- integrity;
- the capacity to act fairly;
- common sense.

These requirements are reassuringly straightforward and easy to recognise as generic professional skills.

Judicial undertakings

Judges and magistrates take two oaths on appointment, the Oath of Allegiance and the Judicial Oath. The Oath of Allegiance for someone who is Christian or Jewish is:

> I, [name], *do swear by Almighty God that I will be faithful and bear true allegiance to Her Majesty Queen Elizabeth the Second, her heirs and successors, according to law. So help me God.*

For other faiths a reference to the appropriate name by which God is known, or to the appropriate holy book, is substituted, and those without religious belief may affirm.

The Judicial Oath is:

> I, [name], *do swear by Almighty God that I will well and truly serve our Sovereign Lady Queen Elizabeth the Second in the office of* [whatever the judicial post is], *and I will do right to all manner of people after the laws and usages of this realm, without fear or favour, affection or ill will. So help me God.*

The important aspects of the Judicial Oath are, first, that right must be done, not in the abstract, but in accordance with the laws and usages of England and Wales. In other words, judges promise to apply the law. Secondly, the law must be applied independently, *without fear or favour, affection or ill will*. In some countries corruption is a fact of life, even corruption of judges. Fortunately, it is nearly two hundred years since there has been any suggestion of corruption on the part of a judge in England and Wales.

Deciding the law

In many cases the applicable law is not disputed and the disagreement is about the facts to which the law should be applied. Sometimes there is no disagreement about the facts and the debate is about what law should be applied to them. In other cases, there are disagreements about the facts and the law.

Some people think that legal disputes can be resolved by looking up the answer in a book. However, applying the law is not like valuing a second-hand car, when if you know its manufacturer, model, year and mileage, you can discover its value. The law is really a series of principles, and legal decision-making involves assessing how the relevant principles should be applied to the particular facts of a case. A legal dispute is really a dispute about what legal principles should be applied in order to resolve it, which can come about in different ways. There may be a difference between principles deriving from different sources. For example, there may be principles established by the common law, but also a relevant Act of Parliament which has modified the common law principles. There may be a relevant European Regulation which could have influenced the principles. In either type of case, it first has to be decided whether there is any conflict between the different sources of the law. If it is decided that there is, the issue depends on which set of principles or modifications takes precedence over the others.

A fairly frequent source of dispute is where it is suggested that different courts have made conflicting decisions on the same point. Again, the judge's first task is to decide whether there are in fact conflicting decisions, which involves considering what principle was established in each of the relevant cases, known as the *ratio decidendi*, which is the legal reasoning underlying a decision. The argument about legal principles then revolves round whether one case can be *distinguished* from another, on the grounds that the legal principles, and not just the facts, were different.

CASE EXAMPLE

If it was decided in one case that the owner of a dangerous animal had an obligation to ensure that it did not attack people, and the animal in question was a tiger, it might be possible to argue that the same principles applied in another case, where the animal concerned was a lion. Conversely, if it was decided that the tiger's owner had an obligation to keep it in a cage, that legal principle would not necessarily apply equally to the owner of a sheep.

Sometimes different judges make inconsistent decisions about the principles applicable to a particular type of case. If that happens, another judge at the same level is free to choose which one to follow. Alternatively, the judge could decide to follow neither, and make their own decision. However, in that situation it is likely that permission would be given to appeal, so that the matter could be decided authoritatively. More difficult is a case where it is said that a decision of one court has been overruled by a decision of a higher court. Usually, the higher court says that it is overruling the decision of a lower court, if that is what it intended. But it can happen that, while giving a decision on one set of principles a higher court lays down a new set of principles which are inconsistent with the principles, contained in a different series of cases (called a *line of authority*). The question of whether the higher court has by implication overruled the second line of authority will come, initially, to a judge sitting at first instance.

Hopefully we have shown that the resolution of many legal disputes is an intellectual exercise approached in accordance with established principles, and that courts rarely have as much scope for imaginative innovation as some people believe.

Deciding the facts

If there is a dispute both about the facts and about the applicable law, the facts have to be decided (*found*) before the law can be applied. How judges and magistrates decide disputed facts is often shrouded in mystery, which is not helped by the way they explain that they have accepted the evidence of one witness rather than another. If a judge says, *I prefer the evidence of A to that of B*, how has this decision been made?

We will try and dispel some of the mystery.

Evidence of witnesses of fact

The English system of justice attributes something approaching an iconic status to witnesses of fact, especially in criminal proceedings, but in practice this is difficult to understand because there are so many obstacles to accurate recall.

Memory

ACTIVITY **11.1**

- *As you sit reading this, ask yourself what were you doing exactly a month ago?*

- *If you are away from home when you are reading this, at what time did you leave home today?*

- *If you think you know, is that because you looked at the clock as you went out of the door, or is it because you always leave home at the same time?*

The busier you are, and the longer the period since the event, the less likely it is that you will have detailed recollection, without reminding yourself from a note or record made at the time. But, you say, if something important had happened, I would remember that. Perhaps, but in what detail?

- *If you have ever had a car accident, when did it happen?*

- *What was the weather like?*

- *What happened immediately beforehand?*

- *What speed were you going?*

The more recently it happened, the better your memory is likely to be. But the more detail you are asked for, the less confident you are likely to be in your answers.

- *Have you ever driven somewhere and found on arrival that you did not remember how you got there?*

If you arrived safely, you must have paid attention while you were driving, but, despite that, there are often parts of the journey which are just blank.

- *The last time you parked your car, what was the colour of the car beside you?*

- *How about the make and model?*

- *The registration number?*

The chances are that you do not remember any of these, because it was not important to you to remember and your brain made no effort to do so, in order to avoid overload. Our brains have insufficient capacity to keep everything in the forefront of our minds and are therefore selective in the information which they store. It is worth reminding yourself regularly that in professional settings, comprehensive and accurate record-keeping is the only way to overcome the shortcomings of memory.

Perception

When you form an opinion, you do not take account of what you did not see or hear. The football referee does not see the foul that takes place behind his back and so, as far as he is concerned, there has been no foul. Yet his whole perception of the event is false. Errors of perception do not have to be total. A shouted warning in a busy street may not be heard because of traffic noise, yet a witness could truthfully and accurately say *I did not hear anything* and create a false impression that there was no warning. Perception also involves filtering so as to make life less complicated. For example, if you smell burning and you know your neighbour is having a bonfire, you are likely to pay less attention to it than you would normally.

ACTIVITY 11.2

Choose a picture from a magazine which includes at least two people and make up a story about them (what happened before, what the picture portrays, what might happen next), based on your interpretation of:

- *their gender, age, culture and status;*

- *their physical appearance, including hair, weight, posture;*

- *their facial expressions;*

- *their clothing;*

- *their relationship;*

- *their surroundings.*

Now ask a friend or colleague to do the same and note down the similarities and differences in your assessments.

What does this tell you about the nature and effects of perception and the influence of stereotyping?

Judgment and estimation

Next, there are judgments which it is assumed everyone can make, but which actually are difficult.

- How fast is a car travelling?

- How tall is the man at the bus stop?

- How do you make your assessment?

- Because you know how tall you are and he is a bit taller or shorter?

- When you make that assessment, are you standing next to him?

- If not, how far away are you?

In fact, most people cannot make accurate assessments of speeds, heights, weights and distances and, even if they can, they have to remember them in order to give accurate evidence about them. Problems of perception and estimation still exist if instantaneous records are made of what is observed. A verbatim record of an hour-long interview would run to around forty typewritten pages. Most case recordings are of one or two pages, which means that a lot of what happened is left out. However, if a record is made, the difficulty over memory is reduced. Don't forget, though, that a delay of a few hours can make a difference, and that perception, judgment and your own physical state will influence what you decide to write.

Assessing truthfulness

So far we have looked at the difficulties an honest witness has in giving accurate evidence. How do you tell who is being untruthful in giving evidence or, indeed, on any other occasion? We are probably all accomplished liars at one level. Think of those gifts you have enthused over, or how frankly you have answered questions about someone's appearance. This sort of social untruth is common, and you may think that there is a difference between little white lies and deliberate intention to deceive, but both are told with the hope and expectation that they will be believed. What it really comes down to is what different people are prepared to be untruthful about and how good they are at doing it. Anecdotal evidence suggests that lawyers and judges are not much better at detecting liars than anyone else. So how do judges decide whether evidence is accurate or not?

Documentary evidence

Leaving aside the possibility of forgery, fortunately rarely encountered, documents produced at the time of the events in question usually give the best idea of what actually happened. The sooner after the event a record is made, the more accurate it is likely to be, which is why your case records are so important. If they are detailed, objective and compiled promptly, there is a good chance that a court will regard them as accurate accounts of the events concerned. In cases with a significant amount of contemporaneous documentary material, courts are likely to accept as accurate evidence which matches the documents. Most business transactions are well-documented in correspondence and e-mails and so, in ordinary civil litigation, there is usually a fair amount of documentary material for the court to consider. In complex commercial litigation, witnesses often do not have, and do not pretend to have, any real recollection of events other than that prompted by the documents produced at the time, which is why in many commercial disputes there is no real argument about the facts.

Assessing witnesses of fact when there are no, or few, documents

Without the support of documents, the process of assessing evidence becomes potentially more complicated. The likelihood of there being no, or few, documents is greatest in criminal cases, when either the jury or magistrates have to decide which facts to accept. Judges who have to choose between conflicting evidence of witnesses of fact, when there are no documents to assist, have a difficult task. The main advantage which they have over anyone else is experience. Qualities such as consistency, grasp of detail, apparent willingness to assist and standing up to cross-examination will enhance a witness's credibility. There is obviously a risk that judges will get the assessment of witnesses wrong, but the system recognises that their assessment is as likely to be as accurate as anyone else's by making it almost impossible to appeal against judges' assessment of witnesses.

Expert evidence

When dealing with children, the court needs all the help it can get. (Butler-Sloss LJ, in Re M & R (Child Abuse: Evidence) [1996] 2 FLR 195)

The court's task in assessing expert evidence is different from making an assessment of the evidence of witnesses of fact. It is most unlikely that there will be any question of the expert being untruthful. Often, experts do not give evidence of facts at all, although that will probably not be so in your case. Judges do, however, frequently have to decide between different expert opinions, and the Court of Appeal has made it clear that they must give reasons for not accepting any expert evidence. Judges differ in how they approach the evidence of experts, and quite a lot depends on how familiar they are with the particular area of expertise. Although some judges are familiar with professional skills other than those of the law, many are not. However, as a result of practice in a particular field, for example family law, some judges become familiar with experts in that area and feel able to evaluate their evidence. But what about unfamiliar areas?

In some types of case, where the issue was essentially one of valuation, judges used to be expected to reach a decision mid-way between what the opposing experts contended. However, now there is usually a single joint expert in such cases rather than experts on opposing sides, and so the need to split the difference has largely gone. In other cases, where compromise is not necessarily appropriate, judges therefore have to grapple with expert evidence and decide which opinions to accept. So how is this done? There are basically two methods:

- concentrating on qualifications, expertise and presentation;
- trying to get into the substance of the expertise.

Trying to understand an unfamiliar area of expertise, to a level which enables you to decide who is right and who is wrong, can seem daunting. However, in practice most of us regularly do this in one way or another.

ACTIVITY 11.3

If two doctors, A and B, are expressing different views about a personal medical matter, how would you decide which to accept? Which of the following factors would influence you most?

- *Dr A is about fifteen years older, and has been in practice as a doctor for considerably longer than Dr B.*
- *Dr B has got postgraduate qualifications, which Dr A has not.*
- *Dr A has only worked in the relevant specialism for a few months, while Dr B has five years' experience.*
- *Dr A is confident in his manner and seems to have a good grasp of the case, whereas Dr B seems rather hesitant and nervous.*

- *Dr B has provided some research findings to back up his opinion.*

- *Dr A is more optimistic about the situation than Dr B.*

- *Dr B is inclined to use jargon, while Dr A is clear in his use of language.*

- *Dr B has considered several possible options, whereas Dr A only seems to have considered one course of action.*

Now consider whether a judge is likely to approach it any differently from you.

The best way to be a helpful witness is to try to understand the task facing the magistrates or judge.

Essentially, judges are likely to feel that any area of expertise should be capable of being explained to someone of reasonable intelligence who is prepared to make the effort to understand, so that if the basis for an opinion cannot be explained with sufficient clarity for the judge to understand, they are likely to reject the opinion, however eminent the person putting it forward. Of course, while trying to understand why experts hold different views, it may become apparent that experience and qualifications are a factor. However, this is different from simply going with the more experienced or better-qualified expert without understanding what the expert issues are. Everyone needs to be careful about being swayed by someone who is good at presentation. We have all come across plausible presenters who rely on work which has been done by others and who, if challenged, cannot demonstrate essential elements of the expertise they claim to have.

Burden of proof

So far we have said nothing about burden of proof. This may surprise you, but in practice it is not as important as you might think. Of course, for a court to make a decision, the evidence needs to cover everything necessary for a case to be made out, or a defence established. Proof beyond reasonable doubt, or proof which makes you feel completely sure, is really only required when juries or magistrates are trying criminal cases. If a key element is not covered by evidence, then there is no proof in respect of that element and the case fails. The burden of proof is also theoretically important in a case where a parent has been acquitted in a criminal court for an offence against a child, and the local authority is seeking a care order based on the same facts. Acquittal of a charge where the burden of proof is beyond reasonable doubt does not mean that a care order cannot be obtained in civil proceedings, where the burden of proof is the balance of probabilities.

The different levels of proof are not very important in making many legal decisions, because of how evidence is presented. As we have seen, it does not often happen in civil or family cases that the only evidence is that of witnesses of fact. If there are contemporaneous documents which support the witnesses, the evidence is usually proved at least on a balance of probabilities, and probably beyond reasonable doubt. On the other hand, if there are no supporting documents, and the court is not satisfied that the factual evidence is accurate, the case for the party whose evidence, has not been accepted fails. It would not be a case of accepting the evidence, but deciding that it did not make the threshold of a balance of probabilities; it would not be accepted at all. The only situation in which the burden of proof might be important is if the judge is thinking: *Well, this might be correct, but then again, it might not*, when the burden of proof can tip the balance.

Appeals

Appeals in ordinary civil cases

In ordinary civil cases it is not possible to appeal against a County or High Court decision without permission, unless the appeal is against a committal order, a refusal to grant habeas corpus, or a secure accommodation order made under the Children Act 1989, s. 25. Applications for permission to appeal are made either to the court making the original order, or to the court to which an appeal can be made. However, if the court making the original order refuses permission, you can apply to the court which has jurisdiction to hear the appeal. Permission to appeal is not given unless the court considers that the appeal has a real prospect of success, or there is some other compelling reason why the appeal should be heard. It is possible to give permission to appeal which is limited to specified issues.

The *real prospect of success* criterion for obtaining permission to appeal means that most cases finish at the trial stage. It is unlikely that permission would be given to appeal in any case which depends simply upon the facts which the judge found. There is obviously a better chance of success in obtaining permission if there is an issue of law. You would expect that judges would not grant permission to appeal unless they thought that their decision on a question of law might be decided differently by the higher court. However, almost every disappointed litigant, at least in the High Court, seeks permission to appeal from the trial judge, whether there are sensible reasons for it or not. If permission to appeal is granted, the appeal is normally a review of the lower court's decision. The appeal court does not usually hear any oral evidence, or any evidence which was not put before the lower court, although there is power to do so exceptionally. The appeal court will not allow an appeal unless the original decision was wrong, or it was unfair because of a serious procedural or other irregularity in the proceedings.

Appeals against decisions of County Court district judges are heard by circuit judges in the same court. Appeals against decisions of County Court circuit judges are usually heard by a single High Court judge, but in multi-track cases they are heard by the Court of Appeal. The Court of Appeal Civil Division also hears appeals from the High Court. Applications to the Court of Appeal for permission to appeal are dealt with by a single Court of Appeal judge. Actual appeals are heard by a panel of two or three judges, usually Court of Appeal judges. In rare cases it is possible to appeal from a decision of the Court of Appeal to the House of Lords.

Appeals in family cases

Appeals in family cases, like appeals in ordinary civil cases, are usually by way of review and not a rehearing. Fresh evidence can be heard on an appeal only in limited circumstances. In family cases it is recognised that whatever decision the court reaches is unlikely to be completely satisfactory, but that it is unlikely that any other decision will be demonstrably better. Consequently, the court's decision should stand unless the conclusion is plainly wrong. The system of appeals from County Courts and the High Court in family cases is similar to that in other civil cases. The Crown Court has no jurisdiction in relation to civil matters and so appeals from the family proceedings court go to a Divisional Court of the Family Division, which comprises two High Court judges.

Appeals in criminal cases

There are two ways in which to appeal against a magistrates' court decision:

- The most straightforward way is to appeal to the Crown Court, if the grounds are that the magistrates reached the wrong conclusion on the facts, or imposed a sentence which was excessive. There is a right to appeal without permission, and the case is heard by a circuit judge sitting with two magistrates. Evidence is heard again, in effect in a second trial, but the risk for an unsuccessful defendant is that the sentencing powers are those of the Crown Court and the sentence could be increased.

- If it is felt that the magistrates' court has come to an incorrect conclusion of law, an alternative means of appealing is by way of case stated to a Divisional Court of the Queen's Bench Division of the High Court. The magistrates have to set out the facts which they have found and the question or questions of law which arose. The arguments are essentially about the correctness or not of the law which the magistrates applied to the facts and there is no right to challenge the facts found. The Divisional Court can determine what the law actually is, and can modify the magistrates' decision in order to reflect that. However, if the defendant wishes to challenge both the facts found and the law applied, the appropriate course is to appeal to the Crown Court.

House of Lords

In limited circumstances, there can be an appeal from the Criminal Division of the Court of Appeal to the House of Lords, which usually sits in panels of five or, exceptionally, seven Law Lords, so that a definitive decision can be made. The Constitutional Reform Act 2005 provides for the creation of a new Supreme Court to replace the House of Lords, and it is planned that serving House of Lords judges will transfer to it. The House of Lords is the final court of appeal in England and Wales, and there is no right of appeal to any court outside England and Wales.

How to complain about what happens in court

If you are a party to litigation and feel aggrieved at the outcome, probably the best course is to seek to appeal. Nothing else is likely to provide a remedy for the perceived injustice, although it is worth remembering that in every case there is likely to be at least one party who is not happy with the result. However, if you are not a party, but a witness or someone who is involved incidentally with the case, you cannot appeal. If you feel dissatisfied with the way you have been treated, or the service you have received, all you may be able to do is to complain.

Judges

If you need to complain about any judicial officer, which includes judges, magistrates or tribunal members, you should first contact the Office of Judicial Complaints which is part of the Department for Constitutional Affairs. If you are dissatisfied, the next stage is to complain to the Office of the Judicial Appointments and Conduct Ombudsman.

Barristers

Complaints against barristers go to the Bar Standards Board, where they are first considered by the Complaints Commissioner, a non-lawyer. If it is decided that the complaint is justified, it is referred to the Conduct Committee of the Bar Standards Board which can refer the matter on. Exactly where it arrives depends on whether the complaint is of inadequate professional service, misconduct, or both. The most serious complaints relate to misconduct, which could result in being disqualified from practising as a barrister. A complainant has no right of appeal, but a barrister can appeal in some circumstances to the Visitors, who are High Court judges. If you are dissatisfied with how the Bar Council responds to a complaint, you can refer the matter to the Legal Services Ombudsman.

Solicitors

Complaints against solicitors are dealt with by the Consumer Complaints Service, which is part of the Law Society and is monitored by the Consumer Complaints Board. For various reasons, a fair number of complaints about solicitors are made, often by other solicitors. As a result, the Consumer Complaints Service is a sophisticated operation and if you complain you will first have contact with a complaints executive or their team manager. If they do not resolve the complaint satisfactorily, you can refer it to the Quality and Service Standards Team. However, the ultimate recourse for complaint, as with barristers, is to the Legal Services Ombudsman.

Deep breath ...

You will have realised that there are several layers of possible complaint and progressing through each layer is likely to take some time. The Consumer Complaints Service, which probably has the largest workload, aims to sort out 75 per cent of complaints within six months of receiving them. The aim for acknowledging the first level of complaint is five working days, with a full response within twenty working days. If you progress to the Quality and Service Standards Team, the same process is repeated. Barristers receive fewer complaints, and it used to be said that most of them were from residents of one of HM Prisons. Whether or not that is so, practising barristers are involved in each of level of complaint other than the preliminary assessment. The current arrangements for complaints against judges only started in April 2006, so it is not yet clear how they are working in practice. The upshot of all this, without wishing to be defeatist, could be that, unless something really bad has happened to you, it may be better to take a deep breath and forget it.

C H A P T E R   S U M M A R Y

In this chapter we have explained how courts approach decision-making, how evidence is assessed and how decisions can be challenged and tested through the appeal system. Courts expect to have at least one dissatisfied party, and so to prevent every case going to appeal, there are clear criteria which govern the circumstances in which appeals can be made. We have also explained what to do if it is necessary to complain about anything which happens in court.

WEBSITES

www.judicialcomplaints.gov.uk.
The Office of the Judicial Appointments and Conduct Ombudsman is 8th Floor, Millbank Tower, Millbank, London SWD1P 4QP.

www.olso.gov.uk
Office of the Legal Services Ombudsman.

Chapter 12

Tribunals, panels and inquiries

Introduction

Tribunals and panels (the two names describe basically the same system) provide the means by which people can challenge the decisions of public bodies. Although they are similar to courts, they are usually less formal and make use of relevant specialist expertise. There is the potential for social workers to advise, advocate for and support people at tribunals, as well as undertake a more formal role as in, for example, providing social circumstance reports to a Mental Health Review Tribunal. Inquiries range from internal local authority reviews to those set up by a government department to consider an issue considered to be of national importance.

Tribunals and panels

Take openness. If procedures are wholly secret, the basis of confidence and acceptability would be lacking. Next take fairness. If the objector were not allowed to state his case, there would be nothing to stop oppression. Thirdly, there is impartiality. How can a citizen be satisfied, unless he feels that those who decide his case come to their decisions with open minds? (Sir Oliver Franks, 1957)

The Franks Report led to the setting up in 1959 of the Council on Tribunals which aimed to ensure that tribunals:

- were accessible to all;

- were quick, informal and as cheap as possible;

- provided the right to an oral hearing in public;

- gave reasons for their decisions;

- were seen to be independent, impartial and fair to all.

In 2001, a review by Sir Andrew Leggatt into the tribunals system was published which advocated a more enabling approach, in which tribunals should be sensitive to the emotional stress caused by appearing at a tribunal, and try to ensure that applicants understand the procedures and are left with the feeling that they have been fully heard. As a result, a Tribunals, Courts and Enforcement Bill is before Parliament which, if passed, will establish a new statutory framework incorporating an Administrative Justice and Tribunals Council in place of the Council on Tribunals, with the following additional functions:

- keeping under review the performance of the administrative justice system;

- reviewing relationships between various components of the system;

- identifying priorities for, and encouraging the conduct of, research;

- providing advice and making recommendations to the government on changes to legislation, practice and procedure which will improve the workings of the administrative justice system.

In April 2006 the Tribunals Service, an executive agency of the Department for Constitutional Affairs, was set up to progressively take over responsibility for providing administrative support to the main government tribunals.

Over 80 tribunals have been established under various Acts of Parliament, usually because specialist knowledge is required to deal with particular types of dispute. Some types of tribunal will be very busy, while a few may sit only very occasionally. If a tribunal has the power to determine a particular type of dispute, usually a court does not have jurisdiction to deal with the same matter. There is no coherent system of appeals, but it is generally possible to seek judicial review if it is suggested that a tribunal has acted unlawfully. In some cases, for example Employment Tribunals, there is an established system of appeals which feeds ultimately into the mainstream system at Court of Appeal level. In other cases there is a right of appeal to a court at a lower level and in some there is no appeal at all.

The new Bill is intended to create a more coherent system of tribunals and appeals by means of First-Tier and Upper Tribunals, with one set of rules covering all tribunal proceedings. In due course, most of the existing tribunals, except Employment Tribunals and Asylum and Immigration Tribunals, will be incorporated into a single First-Tier Tribunal system, from which there will be an appeal on a point of law to the Upper Tribunal. It is expected that tribunal members will be appointed to the First-Tier as a whole, but will not be expected to undertake work outside their area of expertise. To facilitate this, the First-Tier

Tribunal will be grouped into chambers, headed by a chamber president, according to the types of decision required. Legal members of existing tribunals will be appointed to the First-Tier Tribunal and will become known as tribunal judges, responsible to the Senior President of Tribunals. In future, the appointment of tribunal members will be overseen by the Judicial Appointments Commission.

There is currently no means of enforcing directly a tribunal decision. For example, if the Employment Tribunal awards someone a sum of money as compensation and the money is not paid, the only means of redress open to them is to apply to the County Court for the order to be enforced as if it were a County Court judgment. However, this will change if the provisions of the new Bill are enacted.

For social workers, the most significant tribunals in the current system are likely to be Mental Health Review Tribunals, which deal with applications from patients compulsorily detained in hospital under the Mental Health Act 1983 to be released, and Social Security and Child Support Tribunals, which are concerned with entitlements to the range of state benefits, including social security, tax credits, child support, housing benefit and council tax benefit. Other tribunals which you may come across are the Criminal Injuries Compensation Panel, the Special Educational Needs and Disability Tribunal, to which parents can appeal against assessments of special educational needs made by a local education authority, and the Care Standards Tribunal which, among other things, hears appeals from people who have been placed on a list of those considered unsuitable to work with children or vulnerable adults, or who have been refused registration as social workers by the General Social Care Council. All of these tribunals are expected to be incorporated into the First-Tier Tribunal.

Most tribunals currently comprise three members, chaired by a lawyer. The other members are usually a person with relevant professional expertise (such as a psychiatrist for a Mental Health Review Tribunal, or a surveyor for the Lands Tribunal), and a third person, often referred to as a lay member, but who in most cases is required to have some relevant knowledge or experience. In the case of a Mental Health Review Tribunal, the third member is required to have *such experience in administration, such knowledge of social services or such other qualifications as the Lord Chancellor considers suitable*, and the third member of a Disability Benefit Appeal Tribunal should be someone who is *experienced in dealing with the needs of disabled persons in a professional or voluntary capacity, or who is disabled*. In practice, retired social workers are often appointed as lay members of Mental Health Review Tribunals. Some tribunals also make use of assessors to give expert opinion or advice in specialist areas.

Tribunals are intended to offer a quicker and more informal way of resolving disputes, with cost also obviously a significant factor. However, the variety of types of tribunal and the large number of people who sit as tribunal members, has led to concern about consistency in decision-making which potentially impacts on public confidence in the system. One of the objects of the new Bill is to address this issue.

> *We went to hear a case the day before and it was fine, it was all relaxed, and we thought, it's going to be fine, so we weren't prepared for ours to be not so fine.* (Applicant to Employment Tribunal)

Some of the areas in which tribunals operate are quite complex and publicly funded legal assistance is not available, other than for the Mental Health Review and Immigration Appeal Tribunals, which means that many applicants are unrepresented, or rely on organisations such as the Citizens' Advice Bureau or special-interest advocacy groups to advise or represent them. This places a big burden on what are often small organisations, with many demands on their resources.

As tribunal hearings, like court hearings, are essentially adversarial rather than inquisitorial, tribunal chairs often find that they have to intervene in order to assist unrepresented applicants with their cases, to achieve a fairer balance, or to avoid too much damaging confrontation. The Council on Tribunals is actively obtaining the views of users of tribunals in respect of how support to them could be improved, and whether there is scope for developing alternative dispute resolution techniques to reduce the number (and, of course, the cost) of full tribunal hearings. However, the fact remains that many people are daunted at the thought of becoming involved in any judicial process and would welcome informed advice and support.

> *I really don't think any tribunal is suitable for a layman like me. My solicitor did all the talking and I did not speak at all because it was way over my head.* (Applicant to Social Security and Child Support Appeals Tribunal)

Where do tribunals take place?

The rooms used for tribunal hearings are very varied. Some, like Employment Tribunals, sit regularly in designated premises. Mental Health Review Tribunals take place in hospitals, because the applicants are asking to be discharged from compulsory detention. There are no formal tribunal rooms and a meeting room or office at the hospital is made available for hearings. Whether or not there are designated rooms, most tribunal hearings are relatively informal, although some may be conducted more like a court, especially if the nature of the business of the tribunal means that there are likely to be opposing sides – as, for example, in an Employment Tribunal. The degree of formality is usually reflected in the layout of the rooms used. The members of the tribunal usually sit at a table at one end of the room and there may also be a clerk in attendance. There is usually a small gap between the table at which the members of the tribunal sit and the tables, or sometimes just a row of chairs, provided for the other people attending, who sit facing the members of the tribunal. If there are identifiable separate parties, they sit at separate tables opposite the tribunal members. In Mental Health Review Tribunal hearings there are not really opposing parties and so there is no need to distinguish between different sides. There are usually seats for other interested people who wish to attend, such as members of the patient's family in a Mental Health Review Tribunal, or the public in an Employment Tribunal hearing. If witnesses are to give evidence, a separate chair, usually with a table, is provided between the table occupied by the members of the tribunal and the other parties in the hearing.

Social circumstances reports in mental health review tribunals

> *I have seen many social workers at hearings. Most only seem to want to tell me what is not available for a patient if discharged. The one or two who stick in my mind are those who were both realistic and proactive in seeking to facilitate the release of a patient who needed supervision, but not continued detention.* (President of Mental Health Review Tribunals)

Social circumstances reports have a key role in the decision-making process in Mental Health Review Tribunals and what should be included in these reports is contained in the Mental Health Review Tribunal Rules 1983. The Department of Health has also produced guidance notes, and these in combination mean that the social worker faces the same risks as those we identified in Chapter 7, namely that in having to meet such proscribed requirements, there is little room left for analysis and professional opinion, which is usually what the tribunal wants to hear.

Inquiries

This description covers a range of investigative hearings which can take place outside the court system, usually to investigate an apparent failure of systems or procedures, or to respond to complaints. Except in the case of the first type of inquiry, and the second stage of the fourth type, inquiries have no legal powers and depend on the co-operation of those asked to take part.

There are several types of inquiry:

- *Inquiries ordered by a minister*, such as the inquiry set up under the chairmanship of Lord Laming to look into the actions of the agencies involved in the life of Victoria Climbié. They are conducted like court hearings, are often held in public and have the power to require the attendance of witnesses and the disclosure of any information considered relevant. The social work team manager who refused to appear in the Laming Inquiry was ultimately convicted of a criminal offence. Witnesses can be cross-examined on their evidence, as in a court, and the parties are often legally represented.

- *Inquiries set up by a local authority*, usually chaired by an independent person and often held in private. Their remit will depend on the nature of the inquiry and the resources made available for it.

- *Inquiries or reviews which involve one or more agency*, such as those initiated by former Area Child Protection Committees or its successors, Local Safeguarding Children Boards.

- *Complaints against local authorities*, which are handled in two stages. The first takes place internally and, if the complainant remains dissatisfied, the Commission for Social Care Inspection can investigate the eligibility of the case for independent review This may further involve the local government ombudsman or, if the CSCI's actions are considered unsatisfactory, the Parliamentary Ombudsman.

C H A P T E R S U M M A R Y

In this chapter we have looked at tribunals, which supplement the court system as a means of resolving disputes and which are likely to have a continually expanding role in relation to matters within the broad sphere of social welfare. Significant reforms to the present system are currently being proposed and the fact that legal aid is not available for most tribunals means that social workers and advocates are likely to find themselves more closely involved with this aspect of the judicial process in future.

FURTHER READING

Department for Constitutional Affairs (2001) *Tribunals for Users – One System, One Service: Report of the Review on Tribunals by Sir Andrew Leggatt*. London: Stationery Office.

This report, also available on **www.tribunals-review.org.uk**, provides a comprehensive and user-focused review of the tribunals service. However, as we have seen, significant reform is underway.

WEBSITES

www.council-on-tribunals.gov.uk
The Council on Tribunals publishes regular newsletters on its website.

www.dca.gov.uk/legalsys/tribunals
The Tribunals Service.

Chapter 13

Advice and representation in court

Introduction

The conduct of all litigation has been affected by recent changes in the availability of publicly funded legal assistance. This is still available in criminal cases, but over the last few years the government has progressively introduced measures intended to contain the size of the annual legal aid bill. However, overall costs continue to increase due to the rising demands on the criminal legal aid budget, despite the fact that the amount spent on civil legal aid, including family cases, has reduced. As a result of these measures, increasingly, people who need legal advice or who are involved in court proceedings must consider alternative ways of obtaining legal services.

Public funding of legal costs

The administration of the publicly funded system of legal aid is undertaken by the Legal Services Commission, which describes its role as *providing information, advice and legal representation to help about 2 million people each year get access to justice*. The Commission, with a budget of over £2,000 million, is responsible for establishing, maintaining and developing two separate services: the Community Legal Service which provides legal aid in civil cases in so far as legal aid is available in those cases at all, and the Criminal Defence Service which helps people who are under police investigation or facing criminal charges.

Civil cases

Public funding for ordinary civil litigation has almost disappeared and is only available to people whose financial resources do not exceed those prescribed by the relevant regulations. The financial limits differ according to the type of legal advice or assistance sought, and the calculation of eligibility is complicated. Generally financial limits are low, although they are adjusted upwards periodically broadly in line with inflation. Quite apart from the low income and capital thresholds which, if exceeded, mean that there is no entitlement to legal aid at all, the total budget of the Community Legal Service is limited to the amount which the Lord Chancellor decides is appropriate. The Legal Services Commission Code sets out the criteria used to decide whether to provide funding, which include:

(a) *the likely cost of funding the services and the benefit which may be obtained by their being provided;*

(b) *the availability of sums in the Community Legal Service Fund for funding the services and (having regard to present and likely future demands on that Fund) the appropriateness of applying them to fund the services;*

(c) *the importance of the matters in relation to which the services would be provided for the individual;*

(d) *the availability to the individual of services not funded by the Commission and the likelihood of his being able to avail himself of them;*

(e) *if the services are sought by the individual in relation to a dispute, the prospects of his success in the dispute.*

What this comes down to is that the government has limited the funding available for civil legal aid and has decided that restrictive criteria should be applied in deciding how to spend that money, even if the person applying for legal aid satisfies the financial criteria of eligibility.

Family cases

In family cases legal aid is currently available for proceedings under the Children Act 1989, ss. 31, 43, 44 or 45, to a child who is the subject of those proceedings and a parent or person with parental responsibility for the child. Solicitors must be on the Law Society's approved Children Panel, which has branches covering solicitors approved to represent children, adults and local authorities respectively in public law family proceedings, in order to receive public funding. In other types of family case the usual civil legal aid rules apply, except that conditional fee agreements (see below) are not permitted, so that the potential obstacle to the grant of legal aid that it might be possible to enter into a conditional fee agreement does not apply. A large part of the Community Legal Service's budget is committed to family cases, particularly those affecting children, which means that less money is available for other civil cases.

Criminal cases

In criminal cases legal aid is available if a court, or the Legal Services Commission, decides that it is in the interests of justice for the defendant to be represented. The factors taken into account include:

> (a) *whether the individual would, if any matter arising in the proceedings is decided against him, be likely to lose his liberty or livelihood or suffer serious damage to his reputation; ... and*

> (c) *whether the individual may be unable to understand the proceedings or to state his own case.*

Most defendants are likely to satisfy the condition that the interests of justice require that they be represented, and where a right of representation was granted, legal aid used to be free of charge in the first instance. However, except in relation to representation in a magistrates' court, the court trying a defendant could order them to contribute towards their legal costs: if they had not been acquitted (unless there were exceptional circumstances); if they had not been committed to the Crown Court for sentence; if they had not appealed to the Crown Court against a sentence imposed by a magistrates' court; and if it was reasonable, having regard to their resources and the circumstances of the case, including any other financial order made, to make an order in the amount which the judge decided. Criminal legal aid in a magistrates' court was free in any circumstances.

Alternatives to public funding

If civil legal aid is not available, apart from paying for legal advice and representation privately or obtaining it from a trade union or professional association, the principal options in terms of getting legal advice and representation are as follows:

- *Conditional fee agreement* This is an arrangement whereby legal advisers agree not to charge a fee for their services unless the claim in question is successful. They are not permitted in criminal or family proceedings. This is fine as far as it goes, but in most civil litigation, the losing party has to pay the successful party's costs. Under a conditional fee agreement, therefore, an unsuccessful party is still liable to pay the other party's costs, whereas a losing party who is legally aided only has to pay costs to the extent that he can afford to.

- *Post-event legal expenses insurance* This is an insurance against legal costs obtained in return for a premium. The terms of such insurance vary, but it usually only covers a party's own legal costs, rather than any costs which they might have to pay to the other party if they lose.

Conditional fee agreements and post-event legal expenses insurance both amount to gambling on the outcome of litigation. It is true that this is the seasoned bet of the regular punter rather than the traditional flutter on the Grand National, because lawyers who are willing to consider a conditional fee agreement first assess whether the case is likely to succeed, as do post-event legal expenses insurers. However, the outcome of litigation is rarely guaranteed, and so there is always an element of risk. Many lawyers will not undertake work on a conditional fee basis, because they are sufficiently in demand not to have to run the risks of doing work for which they may not be paid.

Pro bono arrangements

One of the fundamental principles of the legal profession is the belief that legal advice and assistance should be available to everyone who needs it, which has prompted some lawyers to accept work on a *pro bono* basis. *Pro bono* is short for *pro bono publico*, meaning *for the good of the public*. The theory is that, as it is in the public interest that legal advice and assistance be given, the work is not charged for. However, as it is voluntary work, it is down to individual barristers or solicitors whether they are prepared to accept work on this basis. The principle that barristers are obliged to act for any client who wishes to engage them is subject to the exception that they do not have to take on work for nothing.

Fixed-fee interview

Some solicitors offer a time-limited interview, either free or for a fixed fee regardless of income, which can be useful if you want to know whether you have a case worth defending or pursuing.

Changes in legal aid

Legal Aid Reform: The Way Ahead was published jointly by the Department for Constitutional Affairs and the Legal Aid Commission (2006) following the recommendations contained within Lord Carter's review of legal aid. A key recommendation of this review was to change the basis of payment for criminal legal aid from the traditional system of hourly rates to one of best value tendering, based on quality, capacity and price. There are plans for a Preferred Providers Scheme and a unified contract for civil legal services, whether provided by law firms or not-for-profit agencies, revised fees for magistrates' court work to take account of travelling and waiting, and fixed fees for police station work. Reading not very far between the lines, you will see that saving money is at the heart of the proposed reforms.

From October 2006 all rights to criminal legal aid, other than legal advice to people detained in police custody, became subject to means testing, even in a magistrates' court. The time taken by the means-testing process, however, soon led to concerns that people were being left unrepresented in court, even in situations where a prison sentence was likely. Also, some lawyers, who provided representation without the means-testing decision having been made, feared that ultimately they would not get paid, or that when they were, it would be less than the economic rate. The New Policy Institute (www.npi.org.uk) has estimated (*Daily Telegraph*, 4 January 2007) that the further reforms proposed will result in three-quarters of adults in working households, and some lone parents on the minimum wage, being ineligible for legal aid in magistrates' courts. The fear is that, unless the scheme is modified, many lawyers will give up legal aid work altogether, leaving many people unable to access legal services.

RESEARCH SUMMARY

The study of publicly funded private law family cases by Kemp et al. (2005) found that the average legal costs incurred in each case was £3,654. Delay and repeat applications were more likely in legally aided than privately funded cases, and costs and delays increased markedly between 1998 and 2004.

Law centres

Law centres, which first appeared in the 1970s, are community-based organisations which employ lawyers who specialise in providing independent legal advice and representation in the general area of social welfare law, including housing, debt, employment, discrimination, immigration and welfare benefits, but not usually family work. Although they operate on the same basis as private solicitors' practices, they are non-profit-making and receive funding from central and local government, trusts and charities. As a result, they may be able to help clients who are not eligible for public funding. The distribution of law centres is patchy, and they tend to operate in socially excluded inner-city areas.

Citizens' advice bureau

This well-known registered charity, with over 3,000 branches, *helps people resolve their legal, money and other problems by providing free, independent and confidential advice and by influencing policy matters*, primarily through trained volunteers. In 2005/6 the organisation responded to over five million inquiries, of which the most common related to benefits, debt, employment, housing and legal problems.

McKenzie friends

Adults have an absolute right in any legal proceedings to represent themselves if they wish, or, as is becoming more common, if they cannot afford to pay for legal representation themselves. However, only qualified and properly instructed lawyers can represent someone else, whether or not they are related to them, so a parent cannot represent their adult child, for example. Nevertheless, it is recognised that someone acting on their own behalf in legal proceedings (known as a litigant in person) may need a bit of help.

In *Collier* v. *Hicks* [1831] 2 B & Ad 663 at 669 Lord Tenterden CJ said:

> *Any person, whether he be a professional man or not, may attend as a friend of either party, may take notes, may quietly make suggestions, and give advice; but no one can demand to take part in the proceedings as an advocate, contrary to regulations of the court as settled by the discretion of the justices.*

It seems that no one tried to take advantage of the potential opportunity this offered until 1971 when, in a divorce case *McKenzie* v. *McKenzie* heard by the Court of Appeal, it was decided that the trial judge was wrong to have prevented one of the parties, who was acting in person, from having assistance of the type envisaged by Lord Tenterden. Following this decision, the name of the case involved has been attached to the role of someone who helps a litigant in person, now known as a *McKenzie friend*.

Courts can decide whether to allow a litigant to be assisted by a McKenzie friend, who is in theory permitted to do only the tasks described by Lord Tenterden. However, in practice a competent and reasonable McKenzie friend can be of great help to both the litigant and the court, who may allow a McKenzie friend to speak in court even if it is not strictly within the limits of their role. Due to the restrictions in civil legal aid, the prominence of McKenzie friends in court proceedings has increased significantly recently, particularly in cases involving children, which has resulted in a number of Court of Appeal decisions about the nature and extent of their involvement.

CASE EXAMPLES

Re H *(McKenzie Friend: Pre-Trial Determination)* [2002] 1 FLR 39

A father successfully appealed against a judge's ruling that he could not have a McKenzie friend at a contact hearing being held in private.

Re O *(Children) (Hearing in Private: Assistance)* [2005] 3 WLR 1191

The Court of Appeal linked a litigant's right to have a McKenzie friend with the right to a fair trial contained in Article 6 of the European Convention on Human Rights. As a result, there is a strong presumption in favour of a court granting permission for an unrepresented litigant to be assisted by a McKenzie friend.

Social workers can act as a McKenzie friend, which could be particularly useful in tribunals, where legal aid is only available in restricted circumstances. However, a note of caution:

A risk you run in representing someone at a tribunal is that you usually get blamed if the outcome is not what the client wanted. (Independent advocate for older people)

Advocates

> *We are not regarded as professionals ... people ignore you ... sometimes at court the social workers and lawyers do not even say 'good morning' ... it feels really abusive ... I often think that this must be how the client feels.* (Independent advocate for people with learning disabilities)

We have already seen that advocate is a generic term used to describe qualified lawyers who represent people in court. However, advocacy also describes the service offered by individuals and organisations to people who may need help and support in getting their views heard in relation to matters such as housing, finance, relationships, employment, health, complaints and legal issues. The settings in which advocates operate include courts, tribunals, panels and other less formal decision-making areas, such as case conferences and reviews. They also support people living in residential care homes and in the community. Advocacy services tend to be specific to a particular client group, such as people with learning disabilities, older people or looked-after children, and may be wholly or partly user-led, sometimes combining the advocacy role with that of an information resource or pressure group. Although training varies, many advocates have built up considerable expertise in helping people handle legal problems and communicate in legal settings. Bateman (2000, p47) describes the principles of this kind of advocacy, which are similar to those which apply to other professional relationships:

- act in the client's best interests;
- act in accordance with the client's wishes and instructions;
- keep the client properly informed;
- carry out instructions with diligence and competence;
- act impartially and offer frank, independent advice;
- maintain confidentiality.

Despite the expansion of advocacy services, many professionals are still ignorant or wary of their involvement and it can be an isolated role. However, it is important for social workers to understand the potential benefits of advocacy, both because it can support people who cannot easily express their own views, and also because advocacy skills are at the heart of much of the legal and procedural framework of social work practice.

Stages of advocacy

Bateman (2000, p140) summarises the six stages of advocacy as:

- presentation of the problem;
- information-gathering, which requires good interviewing skills;
- legal research;

- interpretation and feedback to the client;

- active negotiation and advocacy, which requires assertiveness, good communication and negotiation skills;

- litigation, which is usually the last resort.

ACTIVITY **13.1**

This activity will enable you to develop skills in using a structured approach to problems, incorporating the principles of advocacy.

Think of a recent situation where you were involved in the interpretation or application of rules or procedures, or the presentation of some else's views.

- *Can you identify these six stages within your own responses or actions and the skills you used at each stage?*

- *If any stages were missed out, could this have affected the final outcome?*

- *How did you evidence the principles of advocacy?*

- *What changes would you make if faced with a similar situation in the future?*

Advocacy work often simply involves making those responsible for decision-making aware of the true facts of a case, so that the rules can be fairly applied. However, even this apparently straightforward process can be extremely time-consuming as in, for example, disputes over housing or social security benefit entitlement.

ACTIVITY **13.2**

To practise the information-gathering and research stages of advocacy, next time you are involved in a problem which relates to rules, procedures or regulations, start by compiling a chronology of the facts.

Next, match this to any available documentary evidence and the relevant rules as you understand them, or as you have researched them.

This will enable you to prepare a diagrammatic representation of any arguments in support of the case (similar to the rationale of the skeleton argument described in Chapter 8).

Court 37

To conclude the chapter on legal representation, we offer an illustration of the way in which English law allows litigants in person to seek justice.

As we have seen, adults have the right to represent themselves in any court, and in the Royal Courts of Justice there is a branch of the Citizens' Advice Bureau to assist anyone who needs help in starting an action or making an application. In the Queen's Bench Division of the High Court, Court 37 is permanently set aside for the hearing of what are said to be urgent applications. Each day there is likely to be at least one litigant in person and there may be several, particularly on Fridays. It can take some time for the judge to discover what the litigant's problems are, and often, if there is a particular grievance against the Queen, or the Prime Minister, or other public figure, there is little the court can do. There are also regular customers, some of whom just seem to want to come in for a chat, and who go off apparently satisfied after explaining to the judge various events which cannot be understood without a background which is never explained. Not all litigants accept the limitations of the court's powers, which is why Court 37, a large Victorian court where the judge is several feet higher and much closer to the door than the litigant, was allocated for this purpose in place of a more open-plan court.

C H A P T E R   S U M M A R Y

We have looked at the changing situation in relation to the public funding of legal costs and also at alternative ways of obtaining legal advice and representation. Advocacy, in its generic sense, is where social work and legal skills overlap, and we encourage you to adopt a structured approach to problems which relate to legal or procedural matters. The principle of universal access to justice, as reflected by the role of Court 37 in the High Court, further illustrates the values shared between law and social work.

FURTHER READING

Bateman, N. (2000) *Advocacy Skills for Health and Social Care Professionals*, 2nd edn. London: Jessica Kingsley.
A very practical guide to the increasingly relevant skill of advocacy in social care settings.

In view of the rapid changes taking place in the funding of legal advice and representation, it is safest to keep up to date with this area by using reliable websites, rather than texts.

WEBSITES

www.barprobono.org.uk
The Bar *pro bono* unit is a charity which helps find free legal assistance from barristers.

www.clsdirect.org.uk
The Community Legal Service website provides free legal factsheets and advice, including a topic of the month and a list of legal services providers who hold the CLS quality mark. It also contains a legal aid calculator.

www.citizensadvice.org.uk and its companion website
www.adviceguide.org.uk
The Citizens' Advice Bureau.

www.family-justice-council.org.uk
The Family Justice Council aims to improve the experience of families and children who use the family justice system.

www.lawcentres.org.uk
The Law Centres Federation.

www.lawworks.org.uk
Lawworks is the operating name of the solicitors' *pro bono* group. It does not take on cases involving crime, family or immigration matters.

www.legalservices.gov.uk

The Legal Services Commission website provides a legal aid eligibility calculator.

www.nyas.net

The National Youth Advocacy Service is concerned with children's rights and the provision of socio-legal services to young people up to the age of 25.

www.opsi.gov.uk

Provides free access to statutes and statutory instruments published since 1988. However, the version of any Act available on this site does not include any later amendments.

Chapter 14
What happens next

Introduction

Social workers often describe their court experience as the most demanding of their career. Sometimes the experience is viewed negatively, but with effective preparation and support, it offers opportunities and challenges which do not arise in other areas of work. After it is all over, we encourage you to reflect on what happened, to help you both personally and professionally, not just to survive, but to develop and thrive. We also urge you to ensure that service users' needs remain central to your practice.

First reactions

ACTIVITY **14.1**

This activity will help you think about the impact on feelings and behaviour which can result from allowing yourself to get caught up in the adversarial process.

It's very satisfying [court work] … and you can't get a better high than coming out of there and saying 'result'! (Social worker, quoted in Beckett et al., 2007)

I think you need to see the court, the barristers and the guardian and all the representatives, as the enemy and go for it … and therefore what will happen is that word will be out on the street, so when they get [an authority x case] they go 'oh no' – that is what I want. (Social services manager, quoted in Dickens, 2006)

Continued

I like the fight. (Social worker, quoted in Beckett et al., 2007)

- *Do you think these reactions to court experiences are understandable?*

- *Do you think they accord with social work values and GSCC codes of practice?*

- *What effect will they have on social workers' relationships with service users after the court hearing?*

- *What effect will they have on future relationships with lawyers?*

- *What effect will they have on the social workers' professional development?*

- *Which, if any, of these comments do you think might be made by lawyers after a case which they had won, or a case which they had lost?*

That first reactions tend to be instinctive is understandable, but for professionals they must be followed by a more reflective response. This is necessary to support any future work needed to re-establish effective relationships and for your own professional development. If there is no opportunity for this to happen, there is a risk that involvement in legal processes will result in overly defensive practice, in which social workers take action to avoid being criticised for not taking action (SCIE, 2005, p173). Social workers need to establish communication with lawyers, both in their own interests and in those of service users. By learning the 'rules of the game' and by developing the skills required, you are not compromising the values of your profession; rather, you are establishing yourself as an equal partner in the court setting, which provides the opportunity to influence events, and also potentially make a difference to the experience of service users. However, specialist knowledge and technical skills are not enough; you also need to develop the confidence and independence of thought to question the origin, organisation and purpose of legal rules, and to critically analyse the social context of our court systems (SCIE, 2005, p16).

We have shown that much legal decision-making revolves around balancing one person's rights or opinions against another's, within a complex framework influenced by a range of principles and sources. The core skills that social workers can contribute to these decisions include:

- *knowledge* – for example, about disability, attachment, loss, abuse or neglect;

- *understanding of ethical practice* – for example, confidentiality, accountability, and promoting service users' choice and independence;

- *skills* – for example, in advocacy, assessment, analysis, research and report-writing;

- *values* – such as honesty, transparency, fairness and commitment to social justice.

Reflection

The action of the mind by which it is conscious of its own operations;
contemplation; to consider meditatively, with the implication of censure.
(Chambers dictionary)

Identified by Schön (1983) as an important component of professional learning, reflection is an essential prerequisite for the cultivation of self-awareness and continuing professional development. Relief leads to relaxation, and it is tempting to avoid further professional demands after involvement in court proceedings. However, it is essential to make time for reflection, supported by effective supervision.

Some ideas to encourage reflection include the following:

- pay attention to fleeting thoughts, particularly out of context;
- seek connections between things which you usually think about separately;
- seek contrasting aspects within a situation which you usually see as integrated;
- place single events within a wider context;
- think about the direction in which current circumstances or assumptions might change;
- think experimentally – 'what if ... ?';
- reframe questions;
- consistently analyse your thinking, preferably with the help of good supervision.

ACTIVITY *14.2*

After any court experience, reflect on how it went:

- *How would you describe your overall experience?*
- *What aspects of your preparation were most useful?*
- *What were you pleased about?*
- *What did you find difficult?*
- *What did you not understand?*
- *What most surprised you?*
- *What do you wish you had done differently?*
- *What do you wish you had known about in advance?*
- *What did you think about the behaviour of others?*
- *What have you learned which will help you in the future?*
- *How will you use this to support and prepare others?*

Developing internal checklists in this way will ensure that every experience can be used productively, both for your own and for others' benefit.

Assertiveness

A central aim of this book is to help you develop confidence in the court setting. Confidence involves feeling more in control and dealing with difficult situations without feeling overwhelmed by anxiety or guilt. Although assertiveness is not traditionally thought of as an essential social work skill, it involves (McBride, 1998, p5):

- behaving in a way which is halfway between aggressive and passive;
- feeling confident about yourself;
- respecting yourself and others equally;
- having clear goals;
- being able to say you don't know or don't understand;
- speaking out for yourself or others;
- making your opinion heard in a way which doesn't harm others;
- listening to others' point of view, even if you disagree;
- not putting others down;
- having confident body language;
- having the widest range of behaviour options at your disposal.

All of these attitudes or skills accord with basic social work principles, in that they are based on respect for yourself and others, and they are particularly valuable in the court setting. They can be developed over the course of your training, and throughout your practice, by continually assessing your strengths, identifying areas for development, and evaluating your practice.

ACTIVITY **14.3**

Think of a time when you have been assertive.

- *What made it possible for you to be assertive?*
- *How did you feel immediately beforehand?*
- *How did you feel at the time?*
- *What skills did you use?*
- *How did you feel afterwards?*
- *How can you use this experience productively in your future work?*

This activity builds on the previous one, in encouraging you to evaluate your thoughts and feelings and to use this to identify your strengths and future developmental needs.

Once you have begun to identify areas for development in relation to assertiveness, there will always be opportunities for you to work on them which do not require any special preparation on your part:

- speaking out at meetings, or in lectures or seminars;

- saying 'no' to unreasonable requests;

- asking for clarification of anything you do not understand;

- prioritising your work by means of an action plan;

- taking action to deal with stress, rather than ignoring it;

- seeking out those whom you find difficult to deal with, with a view to establishing more effective communication;

- using observation to identify a role model.

Taking control of your development in this way is itself empowering and will provide a good foundation for gaining skills which will support you in court work.

The needs of service users

The needs and reactions of people who have been personally, as opposed to professionally, involved in court proceedings are individual and unpredictable (Williams, 1999, p51). While there may be some identifiable patterns, it is wrong to make generalisations. Depending on the type of case, possible responses range from fear, disbelief, shame, anger, guilt, resentment, humiliation or grief, to those of relief or a determination to make positive life changes.

> *At one level the justice system can be understood as the major institutional way*
> *we deal with losses, largely around our expectations of how other people will*
> *behave towards us. These losses range from minor slights, where our sense of*
> *fairness is challenged, to more serious encounters where our homes are invaded,*
> *to severe assaults.* (Dawes, in Thompson, 2002, p174)

Any court experience is likely to involve loss for one or more of the people involved. Potential losses range from those which are severe and permanent, such as the decision to place a child for adoption, to those from which recovery is possible and lessons can be learned, such as the restriction of liberty by means of a community sentence or having a part of your evidence rejected by a court.

ACTIVITY **14.4**

List as many different types of loss as you can which might be experienced by anyone as a result of court proceedings, both civil and criminal, distinguishing between losses which are permanent, those which are likely to be temporary and those about which it cannot be predicted whether they will be permanent or temporary.

You may be surprised by the range and extent of potential losses which can be identified – we can think of more than a dozen.

It is not within the scope of this book to explore different models and theories of loss, analyse variations in cultural needs of people experiencing loss, or explore in detail the range of possible professional responses. However, the knowledge base of social work will help you anticipate possible reactions, which clearly can have implications for working with service users in the aftermath of court proceedings. Extreme reactions to loss are most likely from people who are already under some kind of stress, which is likely to apply to most situations in which you are involved professionally. Reactions to loss can include any of the following, either singly or, as is more likely, in combination:

- a refusal to accept what has happened or a feeling of disconnection with reality, sometimes described as *watching oneself on a stage*;

- blame;

- withdrawal from painful reminders;

- resurfacing of previous experiences of loss;

- feelings of vulnerability and impaired ability to cope with quite minor events;

- physical symptoms, such as lack of appetite or difficulty sleeping;

- loss of interest in social contact, or even a wish to move away;

- guilt;

- anger;

- depression.

These reactions may be observed months, or even years, after the event and an ability to anticipate them is important. For example, a mother who refuses to take part in a planning meeting following a court hearing may be unable to cope at that time with the feelings that it arouses. This does not necessarily mean that she does not want to be involved with her child's future, and her raw emotions are more likely to heal if they are accepted, rather than resisted or ignored. Although initially you may not be in a position to mitigate service users' reactions to any great extent, pain is likely to be exacerbated by lack of thought or foresight. This is illustrated by the next case study, which shows how easily the needs of service users can be overlooked after a court hearing and demonstrates the importance of continuing empathy and sensitivity on your part.

CASE EXAMPLE

A local authority had initiated care proceedings in relation to a nine-year-old boy and his mother accepted the advice she was given that, in the circumstances, it was likely that a care order would be made. However, she courageously gave evidence in court to show that, although she could not look after her son, she cared about what happened to him. Although the judge was kind to her, she found the experience very stressful and afterwards she was extremely distressed. With the support of her solicitor, she sat down outside the court and wrote a letter to her son which did not dispute the decision, but which told him how much she loved him and wanted him to have a happy life. A few weeks later she asked the social worker if her son had received the letter and was told it had been lost.

Although there is not sufficient detail here to enable us to offer a view on how the letter should have been dealt with in the best interests of the child, we do suggest that a grieving mother's heartfelt expression of feelings deserved more respect. If, due to the circumstances of any particular case, you do not feel that any support from you is likely to be effective, at least in the short term, then it is important to consider possible alternatives, rather than leave people to cope alone.

C H A P T E R   S U M M A R Y

After a court case is over, the lawyers are likely to move on to the next case without much of a backward glance. Although courts usually seek to minimise any negative consequences of their decisions, they are used to the fact that most of them will result in at least one dissatisfied party. However, social workers and service users are likely to have to work with the consequences for a considerable time afterwards, and we have explored strategies which will support you and also, we hope, result in a less damaging experience for service users. It is important to remember that social workers are better able to respond effectively if they themselves feel supported and able to talk through their reactions and feelings, and so the ability and opportunity to reflect, and the quality of supervision, are key factors in developing effective courtroom skills.

FURTHER READING

Currer, C. (2007) *Loss and Social Work*. Exeter: Learning Matters.
Explores theoretical models of grieving, loss and change, and their practical application.

McBride, P. (1998) *The Assertive Social Worker*. Aldershot: Arena.
Contains lots of activities designed to develop assertiveness.

Williams, B. (1999) *Working With Victims of Crime*. London: Jessica Kingsley.
Looks at the needs and responses of victims to particular types of crime.

Conclusion

The central theme of this book has been that of building bridges between the law and social work. To achieve this, we have explained legal processes as they relate to courts, explored some of the dilemmas and challenges which you may face when undertaking court work and offered some ideas on how to develop your courtroom skills.

Preston-Shoot (2000) has suggested that competent social work practitioners in legal settings are those who are:

- *confident* – to challenge;

- *credible* – in presenting the rationale for decision-making;

- *critical* – to make their practice and legal rules accessible to those with whom they work, to assess the impact of policies on people's lives and to navigate through questions of ethics, rights and needs; and

- *creative* – in order to exploit the possibilities that legal rules present and to manage the practice dilemmas and conflicting imperatives that the interface between law and social work practice generates.

In encouraging you to develop these skills, we support the premise that what is needed is *a kind of new professional, who understands that middle ground, where law meets social work, and can bring together the principles and values they have in common* (SCIE, 2005, p171). We accept that court proceedings can appear to be something of a game. This is not to deny their seriousness for those involved, but we suggest that many professional decision-making settings are similar in this respect. Case conferences, reviews, adoption and funding panels, planning, network and partnership meetings all involve rules and tactics, the understanding of which is essential in order to take a full part and achieve good quality decisions.

We have shown that the legal profession shares some key ethical principles with the social work profession and that remaining true to the values of your profession will maximise the effectiveness of your role in court. We also encourage you to aspire to the highest possible standards of both spoken and written communication and to regard court work as a unique opportunity where the robustness of your practice and knowing the rules can make a key difference to the experience of service users (SCIE, 2005: p174). We hope that we have been able to equip you with some useful resources, and because the law, like social work, is subject to constant change, these will provide you with a framework for your continuing professional development.

> *Where law meets social work, there may be a new mix of skills that brings together the principles and values of both professions and applies them to the task of developing lawful, ethical social work practice. Service users are keen to witness such a development, and for social workers and lawyers to see themselves as allies in the task of promoting rights and justice.* (SCIE, 2005, p187)

References

Baker, J.H. (2002) *An Introduction to English Legal History*, 4th edn. London: Butterworths.

Ball, C., Preston-Shoot, M., Roberts, G. and Vernon, S. (1995) *Law for Social Workers in England and Wales*. London: CCETSW.

Bar Council (2004) *Code of Conduct of the Bar of England and Wales*, 8th edn. London: Bar Council.

Bar Council (2005) *Guidance on Witness Preparation*. London: Bar Council.

Bateman, N. (2000) *Advocacy Skills for Health and Social Care Professionals*, 2nd edn. London: Jessica Kingsley.

Beckett, C., McKeigue, B. and Taylor, H. (2007) Coming to conclusions: social workers' perceptions of the decision-making process in care proceedings. *Child and Family Social Work*, 12 (1): 54.

Beckett, C. and Maynard, A. (2005) *Values and Ethics in Social Work*. London: Sage.

Bond, T. and Sandhu, A. (2005) *Therapists in Court: Providing Evidence and Supporting Witnesses*. London: Sage.

Bond, C., Solon, M. and Harper, P. (1999) *The Expert Witness in Court: A Practical Guide*, 2nd edn. Crayford: Shaw.

Brammer, A. (2007) *Social Work Law*. 2nd edn. Harlow: Pearson Education.

Brasse, G. (2004) Conciliation is working. *Family Law*, 34: 722–5.

Braye, S. and Preston-Shoot, M. (1997) *Practising Social Work Law*. 2nd edn. Basingstoke: Macmillan.

Brayne, H. and Carr, H. (2005) *Law for Social Workers*. 9th edn. Oxford: Oxford University Press.

British Agencies for Adoption and Fostering (1992) *Developing your Court Skills*. London: BAAF.

Broadbent, G. and White, R. (2003) Identifying underlying principles in social work law: a teaching and learning approach to the legal framework of decision-making. *Social Work Education*, 22 (5): 445–59.

Butler-Sloss, E. (2002) Expert witnesses, courts and the law. *Journal of the Royal Society of Medicine*, 95: 431–4.

Carson, D. (1990) *Professionals and the Courts*. Birmingham: Venture Press.

Children and Family Court Advisory and Support Service *Annual Report 2005–6*. London: CAFCASS.

Civil Justice Council (2005) *Protocol for the Instruction of Experts to Give Evidence in Civil Claims*. London: Civil Justice Council.

Cooper, P. (2006) *Reporting to the Court under the Children Act*. 2nd edn. London: Stationery Office.

Cull, L.-A. and Roche, J. (Eds) (2001) *The Law and Social Work*. Basingstoke: Palgrave.

Currer, C. (2007) *Loss and Social Work*. Exeter: Learning Matters.

Dalrymple, J. (2005) Constructions of child and youth advocacy: emerging issues in advocacy practice. *Children and Society*, 19 (1): 3–15.

Department for Constitutional Affairs (2001) *Tribunals for Users – One System, One Service: Report of the Review on Tribunals by Sir Andrew Leggatt*. London: Stationery Office.

Department for Constitutional Affairs (2005) *A Single Civil Court?* London: Stationery Office.

Department for Constitutional Affairs (2006) *Review of Child Care Proceedings System in England and Wales*. London: Stationery Office.

Department for Constitutional Affairs and Legal Services Commission (2006) *Legal Aid Reform: The Way Ahead*. London: Stationery Office.

Department for Educational and Skills (2006) *Working Together to Safeguard Children*. London: Stationery Office.

Department of Health and Home Office (2003) *The Victoria Climbié Inquiry: Report of an Inquiry by Lord Laming*. London: Stationery Office.

Dickens, J. (2004a) Teaching childcare law: key principles, new priorities. *Social Work Education*. 23 (2): 217–30.

Dickens, J. (2004b) Risks and responsibilities – the role of the local authority lawyer in child care cases. *Child and Family Law Quarterly*, 16: 17.

Dickens, J. (2005) The 'epitome of reason': the challenges for lawyers and social workers in care proceedings, *International Journal of Law, Policy and the Family*, 19: 73–101.

Dickens, J. (2006) 'Care, control and change in child care proceedings: dilemmas for social workers, managers and lawyers. *Child and Family Social Work*, 11 (1): 23–32.

Douglas, G., Murch, M., Miles, C. and Scanlan, L. (2006) *Research into the Operation of Rule 9.5 of the Family Proceedings Rules, 1991*. London: Department for Constitutional Affairs.

Dugmore, P. and Pickford, J. (2006) *Youth Justice and Social Work*. Exeter: Learning Matters.

Elkington, A., Greene, J., Holtam, J., Morgan, G., Shield, G. and Simmonds, T. (2004) *Skills for Lawyers*. London: College of Law Publishing.

Freeman, P. and Hunt, J. (1998) *Parental Perspective on Care Proceedings*. London: Stationery Office.

General Social Care Council (2002) *Code of Practice for Social Care Workers*. London: GSCC.

General Social Care Council (2005) *Specialist Standards and Requirements for Post-qualifying Social Work Education and Training: Children and Young People, their Families and Carers*. London: GSCC.

Home Office (1998) *Speaking Up for Justice*. London: Stationery Office.

Home Office (2000) *National Standards for the Supervision of Offenders in the Community*. London: Stationery Office.

Hopkins, G. (1998a) *Plain English for Social Services*. Lyme Regis: Russell House.

Hopkins, G. (1998b) *The Write Stuff: A Guide to Effective Writing in Social Care and Related Services*. Lyme Regis: Russell House.

Iwaniec, D., Donaldson, T. and Allweis, M. (2004) The plight of neglected children: social work and judicial decision-making and management of neglect cases. *Child and Family Law Quarterly*, 16 (4): 423–36.

Johns, R. (2007) *Using the Law in Social Work*, 3rd edn. Exeter: Learning Matters.

Kemp, V., Pleasence, P. and Balmer, N. (2005) Incentivising disputes: the role of public funding in private law children cases. *Journal of Social Welfare and Family Law*, 27 (2): 125–41.

Larkin, E., McSherry, D. and Iwaniec, D. (2005) Room for improvement? Views of key professionals involved in care proceedings. *Child and Family Law Quarterly*, 17 (2): 231–45.

Law Society (1990) *Solicitors' Practice Rules*. London: Law Society.

Law Society (1999) *Guide to the Professional Conduct of Solicitors*, 8th edn. London: Law Society.

Law Society (2004) *Solicitors' Anti-discrimination Rules*. London: Law Society.

Lindley, B., Richards, M. and Freeman, P. (2001) Advice and advocacy for parents in child protection cases – what is happening in current practice. *Child and Family Law Quarterly*, 13: 167.

McBride, P. (1998) *The Assertive Social Worker*. Aldershot: Arena.

McKeigue, B. and Beckett, C. (2004) Care proceedings under the 1989 Children Act: rhetoric and reality. *British Journal of Social Work*, 34 (6): 831–49.

Mantle, G. (2001) *Helping Parents in Dispute: Child-centred Mediation at County Court*. Aldershot: Ashgate.

Masson, J. and Winn Oakley, M. (1999) *Out of Hearing: Representing Children in Care Proceedings*. Chichester: Wiley.

National Association for the Care and Resettlement of Offenders (NACRO) (2006) *Guide to the Youth Justice System in England and Wales*. London: NACRO.

National Society for the Prevention of Cruelty to Children (NSPCC) (2003) *The NSPCC Review of Legislation Relating to Children in Family Proceedings*. London: NSPCC.

Partington, M. (2006) *Introduction to the English Legal System*, 3rd edn. Oxford: Oxford University Press.

Plucknett, T. (1956) *A Concise History of the Common Law*, 5th edn. London: Butterworths.

Preston-Shoot, M. (2000) Making connections in the curriculum: law and professional practice. In R. Pierce, and J. Weinstein (eds), *Innovative Education and Training for Care Professionals: A Provider's Guide*. London: Jessica Kingsley.

Preston-Shoot, M., Roberts, G. and Vernon, S. (2001) *Values in social work law: strained relations or sustaining relationships?* Journal of Social Welfare and Family Law, 23 (1): 1–22.

Quality Assurance Agency for Higher Education (QAA) (2000) *Social Policy and Administration and Social Work Subject Benchmark Statements*. London: QAA.

Schofield, G. (2004) The voice of the child in public law proceedings: a development model. In M. Thorpe, and J. Cadbury (eds), *Hearing the Children*. Bristol: Jordan.

Schön, D. (1983) *The Reflective Practitioner*. New York: Basic Books.

Smart, C., May, V., Wade, A. and Furniss, C. with Sharma, K. and Stretitz, J. (2005) *Residence and Contact Disputes in Court*. London: Stationery Office.

Smith, C. (1997) 'Mutual respect or mutual distrust: social workers and the courts in child care decisions', *Liverpool Law Review*, 19 (2): 159–79.

Social Care Institute for Excellence (SCIE) (2005) *Teaching, Learning and Assessment of Law in Social Work Education*. Bristol: Policy Press.

Stanley, L. (2004) Children's guardians and the local authority: managing disagreement. *Family Court Journal*, 2 (2) – available at the Family Justice Council website: http://www.family-justice-council.org.uk.

Thompson, N. (ed) (2002) *Loss and Grief*. Basingstoke: Palgrave.

Timmis, G. (2003) Lawyers' perspectives of public law cases. *Family Law*, 33, 174–80.

Tisdall, E., Bray, R., Marshall, K. and Cleland, A. (2004) Children's participation in family law proceedings: a step too far or a step too small? *Journal of Social Welfare and Family Law*, 26 (1): 17–33.

Wall, N. (1997) Judicial attitudes to expert evidence in children's cases. *Archives of Disease in Childhood*, 76 (7): 485–7.

Westcott, H. (2006) Child witness testimony: what do we know and where are we going? *Child and Family Law Quarterly*, 18 (2): 175–90.

Williams, B. (1999) *Working With Victims of Crime*. London: Jessica Kingsley.

Youth Justice Board (2004) *National Standards for Youth Justice Services*. London: Youth Justice Board.

Index